THE
CLASSIC
MEDITERRANEAN
COOKBOOK

SARAH WOODWARD
THE
CLASSIC
MEDITERRANEAN
COOKBOOK

RD
PRESS

MONTREAL

A DORLING KINDERSLEY BOOK

Editor
Lorna Damms

Art Editor
Jo Grey

Designer
Helen Diplock

DTP Designer
Karen Ruane

Managing Editor
Susannah Marriott

Senior Managing Art Editor
Carole Ash

Photography
Clive Streeter
Dave King

Food Stylist
Janice Murfitt

Production Controller
Lauren Britton

Published in Canada in 1995 by
The Reader's Digest Association (Canada) Ltd.
215 Redfern Avenue, Westmount, Quebec H3Z 2V9

The Reader's Digest Association (Canada) Ltd.
is a licensed user of the trademark RD Press

Canadian Cataloguing in Publication Data

Woodward, Sarah
The classic Mediterranean cookbook

Includes index.
ISBN 0-88850-329-6
1. Cookery, Mediterranean.   1 Title.
TX725.M35W647 1995   641.59'1822   C95-900351-7

Reproduced in Singapore by Colourscan
Printed and bound in Italy by A. Mondadori, Verona

95 96 97 98 / 5 4 3 2 1

CONTENTS

INTRODUCTION 6
A HEALTHFUL WAY OF EATING 8

MARKET PRODUCE 10

*A vibrant full-color guide to the key
ingredients used in Mediterranean cooking,
with advice on choosing, preparing, and storing*

Vegetables **12**
Fruit and nuts **16**
Fish **18**
Shellfish **20**
Meat **22**
Herbs and spices **24**
Staple foods **26**
Cheese and yogurt **28**
The pantry **30**

CLASSIC DISHES 32

*Authentic specialties from the eastern and
western Mediterranean, illustrated with
photographs of the finished dishes
and their ingredients*

Zuppa di Pesce **34**
Italian fish soup

Gazpacho Andaluz **36**
Chilled Andalusian soup

Tapas **38**
A selection of Spanish appetizers

Imam Bayildi **40**
Turkish stuffed eggplant

Gnocchi al Pesto **42**
Italian potato dumplings with pesto sauce

Meze **44**
Greek and Turkish dips and snacks

Djej Emshmel **46**
Moroccan chicken tagine

Pissaladière **48**
Provençal onion tart

Grilled food **50**
*Including Moroccan grilled spring chicken
and Turkish lamb kebabs*

Paella Valenciana **52**
Traditional paella from Valencia

Kounelli Stifatho **54**
Greek rabbit casserole

Rougets à la Niçoise **56**
Red mullet Niçois style

RECIPES 58

*Over 120 traditional dishes and modern
interpretations of celebrated classics for colorful
and mouthwatering meals*

Soups **60**
First courses and snacks **66**
Vegetable dishes **74**
Fish dishes **90**
Meat dishes **106**
Pasta, rice, and grains **120**
Preserves **132**
Desserts **134**
MENU PLANNING 140

TECHNIQUES 146

*Special equipment and step-by-step
preparation techniques*

Cooking equipment **148**
Preparing vegetables **150**
Dough and pastry **151**
Fish and shellfish **152**
Meat **154**

NUTRITIONAL INFORMATION 156
INDEX 157
ACKNOWLEDGMENTS 160

INTRODUCTION

The countries of the Mediterranean enjoy a cuisine rooted deep in classical traditions. This, after all, was the sea crisscrossed by the Minoans, Phoenicians, ancient Greeks and Romans, as each built their empires. Then came the Arabs, with their love for gardens and fruits. For centuries the countries bordering this bountiful sea may have suffered under conquering armies, but they also found themselves on major trade routes.

The cooks traveling with these armies and courts brought new ideas for the kitchen. The fish soups that are now found throughout the region are credited to the Greeks, while Arabs taught the Sicilians to make water ices. There is even a theory, hotly disputed, that the Romans were introduced to the art of pasta making by the Chinese. With the precious cargoes from the East and India arrived exciting new foods to supplement the basic crops of wheat, olives, and grapes; not just spices, but citrus fruits, melons, eggplant, peaches, and pomegranates. And if the discovery of the New World at the end of the 15th century led to a collapse in the old trading empires, it did not halt the flow of new ingredients carried back by the different armies – tomatoes, peppers, and beans being some of the most important introductions.

The Mediterranean region has always enjoyed a cross-fertilization of culinary ideas, and the gastronomic borders are still blurred. In Sicily you can eat a fish couscous that bears a remarkable similarity to that served over the water in Tunisia; you can enjoy figs baked in honey in Provence just as well as in Greece. And if there are similarities, there are also constants – wherever you are in the Mediterranean, you will find olives, bread, lemons, herbs, and spices. For wherever those seafaring cooks landed, they found similar growing conditions. Long hot summers and dry winters mean that, despite its apparent lushness in spring, this has always been a harsh region for farmers. As a result, the Mediterranean diet, lacking rich butter, cream, and meat-based dishes, is often described as austere, even sober. To me it is anything but that. Looking at the riot of color in the markets, the bunches of glossy green herbs, the vibrant shades of the fruit, I am instead struck by the abundance of the region. Even in the middle of the arid summer, away from the crowded tourist beaches, the air is heavy with the scent of the herbs growing wild on the hillsides.

The life of the Mediterranean lies in the mountains that rise above the pine groves, in the small hilltop villages and particularly in the busy cities that ring its shore. It is here that you will still find the

kind of meal most of us dream of when we think of the
Mediterranean. You may be sitting on a terrace overlooking the
sea, in a little market café, or in the dark cool kitchen of a friend.
The meal will start with something to nibble with a glass of wine,
perhaps a few olives and some spicy dips served with warm bread.
There may be a pasta dish laden with garlic and herbs, some fish or
meat cooked over charcoal and, to refresh your palate, a bowl of
fresh fruit on ice. If the weather is cooler, you may start with a
thick soup scattered with Parmesan, followed by a casserole laden
with spices, and, to finish, a sticky pastry served with a cup of
steaming coffee.

There is no need to restrict this kind of meal to an idyllic memory.
It is easy to create a Mediterranean meal at home, provided you
obey one basic rule: take care to buy the best quality ingredients in
season. The Mediterranean peoples are great shoppers. This
attribute above all others characterizes the quality of their food.

I have brought together here recipes from throughout the region,
from its very western shores to its eastern limits. They are all my
favorites. For this is food that is good for you, easy to prepare, and
a delight to look at as well as to eat – reflecting the great classical
traditions of the Mediterranean.

A HEALTHFUL WAY OF EATING

The main crops of the Mediterranean have always been wheat, olives, and grapes, and from these core products come the principles of Mediterranean eating. The classic snack is still coarse bread (perhaps rubbed with tomato or garlic), dunked in olive oil, accompanied by a glass of red wine, and followed by fresh fruit.

Nutritionists, after decades of study, have come to believe that this simple diet is directly beneficial. Its merits stem from the heavy emphasis on cereals, fresh fruit, vegetables, and fish and the limited amounts of dairy products and meat eaten. Evidence even appears to indicate that red wine, consumed in moderation, may have a positive effect in the avoidance of heart disease.

OLIVE OIL

The Mediterranean diet results in part from the climate and terrain. This area is not conducive to cattle raising, so olive oil takes the place of butter. High in mono-unsaturated fats and easy to digest, olive oil is believed to be one of the best cooking mediums available. Of course, it should be consumed in moderation, for it has as many calories as other fats and oils.

FRUIT AND VEGETABLES

Fresh vegetables and fruit are important sources of vitamins, and studies have shown that they may even offer protection against certain chronic diseases. In the Mediterranean, most fruit is eaten raw, as part of the daily diet, and vegetables are used in abundance. The typically simple preparation is also beneficial; some vitamins leach out during cooking, but if fresh produce is cooked briefly and served with its cooking liquids, few nutrients are lost. The ubiquitous garlic is an important ingredient as it contains substances that appear to lower blood pressure and cholesterol.

BEANS, PEAS, CEREALS, AND PASTA

Beans and peas are an excellent source of protein, contain iron, and are high in soluble fiber and low in fat. When legumes are eaten with cereals, the combination provides a "complete" protein, as nutritionally valuable as fish or meat, as in Tuscan bean and pasta soup or the rice and lentil dishes of the eastern Mediterranean. Cereals provide the bulk in the Mediterranean diet. The flour that is milled from the local wheat is not too highly refined, giving a unique flavor and consistency to the country-style breads that accompany most meals.

The durum wheat used in pasta is full of proteins and vitamins and so a dish of pasta with a vegetable sauce is both healthy and, because it is high in carbohydrates, sustaining. Durum wheat is also consumed as couscous in North Africa, while bulgur wheat is common to the east of the region. Rice, another staple, is a valuable source of carbohydrates, protein, and B vitamins.

Meat and Dairy Produce

Sheep and goats are the region's main livestock and are as important for their milk as for their flesh. Milk is rarely consumed fresh, but is used to make yogurts and cheeses. Pigs are also farmed and pork is often cured for use in salamis and hams, which are eaten in small quantities. Little is wasted; nutrient-high organ meats are widely used. Poultry, a low-fat meat, is very popular, and lean game is a valued resource. But, like dairy products, meat is as likely to be used as a flavoring as to constitute the main element of a meal.

Fish and Shellfish

Fish is often the central element of a meal and is an important protein source. It is especially useful in "completing" the vegetable proteins provided by cereals – a little fish served with pasta or bread allows the digestive system to get the full benefit from the protein offering. Popular oily fish like sardines and mackerel are rich in essential fatty acids, which help protect against heart disease and promote health generally. The usual way to prepare fish is to broil or bake it, which is also the healthiest approach.

Perhaps, above all, it is the Mediterranean peoples' overall attitude toward food that makes their way of eating so healthy. Food is taken seriously here. Time is spent both in its preparation and consumption, producing well-balanced meals to share with family and friends.

MARKET PRODUCE

One of the great pleasures of being in the Mediterranean is shopping in the markets that dot its shores. The cooking of the region is founded on the seasonal local produce, be it fish fresh from the sea or sun-ripened fruit and vegetables. Many dishes are prepared very simply to allow the flavors to shine through, so the quality of the ingredients is a prime consideration. The Mediterranean cook is above all a discerning shopper.

VEGETABLES

The Mediterranean market is a colorful sight at any time of the year because throughout the region, vegetables constitute a large part of the daily diet. Many vegetables owe their distinctive sweetness to having been sun-ripened and picked in their prime. Produce is used when it is in season and, therefore, when at its most flavorful.

OTHER TYPICAL VEGETABLES
beets, chicory, peas, potatoes (larger floury varieties and small waxy salad potatoes), Swiss chard, grape leaves, cardoons, horta (wild greens)

CUCUMBERS
Small ridged cucumbers have a firmer texture and are the most flavorful. Tiny cucumbers pickle well.

Zucchini blossom

Flat bean

Marmande tomato

Plum tomatoes

Small cucumber

ZUCCHINI
Small zucchini are sweetest; larger fleshy ones can be bitter and should be salted before use. The orange flowers taste delicious fried in olive oil.

TOMATOES
The tomato is central to Mediterranean cuisine. Plum tomatoes should be used for cooking and firm-fleshed Marmande or beefsteak tomatoes in salads — the riper the better. Hothouse tomatoes cannot compete with those ripened in the sun.

Runner bean

BEANS
Fava beans, unless very young, have tough outer skins that should be removed. Long flat beans or runner beans are essential to paella. Choose crisp specimens that are not too long and remove the fibrous strings before cooking. White beans and borlotti beans are eaten fresh in France and Italy.

Fava beans

Radicchio

Romaine

SALAD LEAVES
Mediterranean salads contain an infinite variety of small bitter leaves and sweet herbs, reflecting the variety growing in the wild. Arugula, dandelion leaves, endive, purslane, and mâche frequently appear in salads, while romaine, radicchio, and curly endive are popular larger lettuces.

EGGPLANT

It is difficult to imagine Mediterranean cooking without the eggplant, but when it was first brought from the East, it took many years to become accepted. Choose plump but not overlarge eggplants, with taut, glossy skins, and watch for unusual varieties, such as round white eggplants or the tiny pickling variety.

FENNEL

The dried branches of the wild fennel that grows in the hills surrounding the sea are often used to scent barbecues with their anise aroma. When using the cultivated Florentine fennel, keep the feathery fronds for use as an herb.

Florentine fennel

Green pepper

CELERY

Celery is usually eaten cooked. Look for celery with leaves attached — they are much used in Italian cooking.

Thin green stalks

White asparagus

Red pepper

PEPPERS

Introduced from the New World, capsicum peppers, like the tomato, are today an integral part of Mediterranean food. They range in color and shape from tapering pale green varieties to the dark green and red bell-shaped sweeter peppers.

ASPARAGUS

First cultivated by the Romans, asparagus grows wild in the Mediterranean region. The spindly green stalks of the wild variety are prized by the Spanish, while the Italians prefer luscious fat white asparagus.

Arugula

Curly endive

GLOBE ARTICHOKES

The globe artichoke, like its relative the chard, is a member of the thistle family. Tiny new spring artichokes are tender enough to be eaten whole. The hearts of the larger varieties are a seasonal delicacy.

Mâche

Freshly picked
mushrooms should be
dry with stalks intact

Cèpe

*Horns of
plenty*

*Cultivated
mushroom*

Chanterelles

*Spring
onion*

MUSHROOMS

*Gathering wild mushrooms is akin to a national sport in the
western Mediterranean. The cèpe (porcini), the horn of plenty
(trompette-de-mort), and the chanterelle are highly prized.
Cultivated button and field mushrooms are also widely used.*

BROCCOLI

*This vegetable can be purple or white, as
well as green, which is the variety
known in Italy as* calabrese. *The heads
should be small and compact. It
responds well to quick cooking.*

LEEKS

*Like their relative the
onion, leeks play an
important role as a basic
flavoring in many dishes,
such as vegetable soups, as
well as being eaten as a
vegetable in their own
right. Always wash
and trim leeks before
use, to remove any
traces of grit.*

Leek

*Spanish
onion*

ONIONS

*Large golden-skinned
Spanish onions,
white mild
onions, sweet red
onions, long
scallions, and
tiny pickling onions
are much used in
Mediterranean cooking.
Keep them in a dark place
and discard any that have
started to sprout.*

*Red
onion*

PUMPKINS

Small pumpkins have sweeter flesh than overgrown ones, which can be fibrous. They are popular in savory dishes, as the flavor marries well with rich foods, herbs, and spices.

The tender stalks of baby leaves do not need to be removed

SPINACH

Spinach leaves should be crisp and bright green, with no hint of yellow or sliminess. Cooking, which should be brief, vastly diminishes the bulk of this vitamin-rich vegetable. Baby leaves are good raw in salads.

CARROTS

Large, older carrots are generally preferred for their stronger flavor, especially in the eastern Mediterranean – the exception is if a dish calls for spring vegetables. Carrots should always be crisp and juicy when broken in half; discard any that feel soft or are wrinkled.

CABBAGES

First harvested by the Romans from a sea plant, cabbages are a staple vegetable in the Mediterranean. Look for the cavolo nero, or black cabbage, much used in Tuscany for its distinctive flavor and hue, and the dark green savoy. Red cabbage is a popular winter salad leaf in Turkey.

Romanesco cauliflower

CAULIFLOWERS

Members of the cabbage family, cauliflowers can be found in various colors; vivid green pyramidal florets can be found as well as more typical white formations. Cauliflowers should be firm and even in color – avoid any that are blemished or slightly soft.

Common cauliflower

TURNIPS

New turnips are small, sweet, and tinged with pink. They can be eaten raw in salads or braised and then caramelized and are often found in Moroccan couscous dishes. The Lebanese make a piquant turnip pickle.

Savoy cabbage

FRUIT AND NUTS

Fresh and dried fruit is an essential component of the Mediterranean diet. A selection of chilled fresh fruit is the most typical and delicious way to end a meal; out of season, dried fruit and nuts may be offered. Both fruit and nuts are used in savory and sweet dishes, especially in North Africa and toward the east of the region.

OTHER TYPICAL FRUIT

apricots; cherries; pears, such as comice and conference; tangerines, clementines; persimmons or sharon fruit; bilberries

Wild strawberries

POMEGRANATES

The pomegranate's sour, perfumed juice is used in savory dishes in the eastern Mediterranean.

Mirabelles

Purple plum

STRAWBERRIES

Huge crops of early strawberries are grown in Spain in particular. In Italy and southern France, look for the more aromatic little wild strawberries from the woods.

PLUMS

Eaten both fresh and cooked, plums originated in Europe and are found in many varieties, from tiny sweet yellow mirabelles to large juicy purple plums. In their dried form as prunes, they are used to enrich savory dishes.

PEACHES

If a peach is ripe, its skin will peel away easily; avoid any that are bruised. White peaches and white smooth-skinned nectarines are especially delicious.

LEMONS

Originally from Southeast Asia, the lemon is now a central element of Mediterranean cooking. The juiciest lemons are plump, thin-skinned, and feel heavy for their size. For dishes that require the zest, use unwaxed lemons.

ORANGES

The first orange introduced to the Mediterranean from Southeast Asia was the bitter Seville orange, but today there are many sweet varieties, including Jaffas and Valencias. Blood oranges provide especially good juice for drinking.

Valencia orange

DRIED FRUIT
The glut of fresh fruit is dried for the winter months, when it is used extensively in savory and sweet dishes. Apricots, figs, dates, raisins, and prunes are particular favorites.

Raisins

Pine nuts

Whole almond

Flaked almond

Apricots

Chestnuts

Vermilion seeds make a beautiful garnish

Dates

Walnut

NUTS
Pine nuts, taken from pine cones, are the most distinctive nut in the region's cooking; almonds, walnuts, chestnuts, hazelnuts, and pistachio nuts are also much used. Shelled nuts should be kept tightly sealed and used quickly. Toasting nuts enhances their flavor.

The flesh of the quince is close-grained

FIGS
A plump, ripe fig has an intensely sweet flavor. Avoid cracked or bruised fruit. Bright green, underripe figs are delicious baked.

Juicy white muscatel grapes

Black grapes

QUINCES
A relative of the apple and pear, the quince is a hard, acidic fruit and is always eaten cooked, often in the form of a paste. The Moroccans add quinces to tagines.

GRAPES
If there is a definitive Mediterranean fruit, it is the grape, without which there would be no wine. There are myriad species — grown for wine or the table. Look for tiny black grapes known in Italy as fragoli and muscatel grapes.

Watermelon

APPLES
Cultivated originally from the wild crab apple, eating varieties of this fruit vary enormously. Both fresh and dried apples are sometimes added to Moroccan tagines.

MELONS
The yellow-fleshed Charentais and Galia melons give off a powerful fragrance when ripe, so sniff them at the stalk end before buying. A good melon will also feel heavy for its size. Chilled slices of gorgeously colored watermelon make a refreshing finish to a meal.

FISH

The countries of the Mediterranean have always relied heavily for food on the produce of the sea that links them together. Today the catches have declined, but fish remains a central part of the diet. For me, one of the great pleasures of travel in the area is to sit at a harborside café, watching the local fishing boats landing their catch.

OTHER TYPICAL FISH
brill, John Dory (tilapia), hake, rock fish (the rascasse or scorpion fish, gurnard or sea robin, weever and star-gazer), sole, grouper, bonito, whiting, conger eel

SEA BASS
This firm-fleshed fish is much appreciated for its fine flavor, a fact reflected in its price. Smaller sea bass are best grilled over fennel branches, so the flesh becomes permeated by the aroma, while larger ones have a delicate flavor when poached in a white wine broth.

Smaller sardines have the best flavor

SARDINES
The sardine is a common catch all over the Mediterranean. It is an inexpensive fish and a valuable source of protein. Very fresh sardines wrapped in grape leaves and grilled over charcoal have a unique flavor.

ANCHOVIES
Most of the anchovies landed are taken to be processed and canned, but this delicate, oily fish can sometimes be found fresh in the market.

Fresh anchovies are delicious deep-fried

FISH STEAKS

For the broiler or grill, choose firm-fleshed fish that can be cut into steaks or cubes. Swordfish, which is popular in Turkish cuisine, is a good choice, as is tuna, which has been caught in the Mediterranean since classical times. The ugly monkfish is perfect for kebabs.

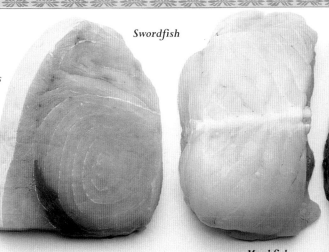

Swordfish

Monkfish

Tuna

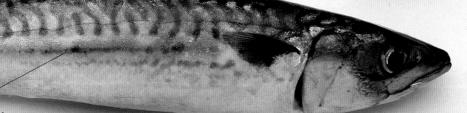

Fresh mackerel has silvery, green-striped gleaming skin

MACKEREL

A strongly flavored fish, mackerel has a high oil content and is particularly suited to being broiled or grilled. To be enjoyed at its best, mackerel must be especially fresh.

SEA BREAM

There are many varieties of sea bream. The best for eating are dentex, a silver fish with light blue spots, and the gilt-head bream or daurade, a fish distinguished by a golden mark on each cheek. It may be cooked whole or cut into fillets.

RED MULLET

The red mullet is one of the most sought-after Mediterranean fish, valued for its exquisite flavor.

Dentex

GRAY MULLET

Growing much larger than the red mullet, the gray mullet is a versatile firm-fleshed fish that is good eaten cold or hot. The roe of the gray mullet is a delicacy used to make Greek taramasalata *and Italian* bottarga, *salted, pressed, dried roe encased in wax.*

Whitebait

SMALL FISH

All manner of small fry are taken from the Mediterranean to be fried in olive oil and eaten as a snack or first course. Whitebait and the transparent goby are especially popular catches.

SHELLFISH

Freshness is an essential quality of good shellfish. Whenever possible, buy fresh raw seafood — translucent pinky gray shrimp and freshly gathered live mussels and clams are delectable ingredients, and in the Mediterranean, even crabs and lobsters are sold live.

OTHER TYPICAL SEAFOOD
razor clams, sea urchins, sea snails, date shells (often eaten raw), ormers (similar to abalone), cockles, winkles, whelks

SCALLOPS
In season, the white muscle of the scallop has an orange coral, or roe, attached. It should be briefly cooked to retain its succulence.

OYSTERS
Now farmed and continuously available, oysters are delicious both raw and lightly cooked. They must be absolutely fresh.

CLAMS
Of the many species of clams and cockles in the Mediterranean, the tiny vongole, or Venus clam, is especially sweet and tender.

Venus clams

Mussels

Large muscle
after cleaning

LOBSTERS
The rock lobster, distinguished by its lack of front claws, is more often found in Mediterranean fish markets than the common lobster. It is highly prized for its meaty tail.

Rock lobster

MUSSELS
These vary in size, according to species. Small mussels are particularly sweet. Avoid mussels with broken or cracked shells.

Spider crab

The claws contain
juicy white flesh

CRABS

The spider crab is named for its long
spindly legs, which contain most of the
meat. It is a popular catch and makes a
dramatic centerpiece to a shellfish platter. The
many different varieties of small crab that are also
landed are much used in fish soups and stews.

Squid

CEPHALOPODS

Squid, cuttlefish, and octopus, all of the
cephalopod family, are widely eaten in the
Mediterranean. Small squid and cuttlefish can
be quickly cooked, but larger squid and octopus
require slow cooking, preferably after being
marinated, to tenderize the otherwise chewy flesh.

Small squid are
tender

Cooked shrimp   *Raw shrimp*

SHRIMP

From tiny brown shrimp to fat pink
Mediterranean ones, there is an endless
variety of these crustaceans. Separate
from this category is the delectable
long-clawed langoustine, or Dublin Bay
shrimp, which is actually part of the
lobster family. If possible, buy uncooked
shrimp — they will typically be a rosy gray,
turning pink only when cooked.

Langoustine

MEAT

The dry climate and the small landholdings typical of the Mediterranean have contrived to make meat a rare resource, to be treated as a luxury, and it is often preserved for times of scarcity. Lamb and pork are more common than beef, and birds of all sorts are eaten. In the cooler months, game is frequently served.

OTHER MEATS:
kid (especially popular in Greece), suckling pig, morcilla (Spanish blood sausage), mutton, pheasant, rabbit, hare, wild boar

DRIED AND CURED MEATS

PANCETTA
The Italian pancetta is the same cut of pork as bacon, cured in salt rather than smoked. The French call this cut petit salé.

Prosciutto

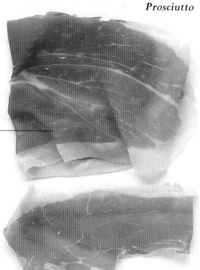

Cured ham is typically thinly sliced

Serrano ham

A finely textured salami with relatively high lean meat content

Salami Milano

CURED RAW HAMS
Whole hams, salted and air-dried, produce delicate meat. The most famous are prosciutto di Parma, *and Spanish* jamón Serrano (Serrano ham).

Salsiccia Calabria

Chorizo

Coarse sausages made from pork and hot spices

CURED SAUSAGES
Best known by their Italian name salami, there are many types of cured sausages, especially in the western Mediterranean. Usually made with pork, they can be highly spiced or quite mild, intended to be eaten as they are or used in cooking, like the two varieties of Spanish chorizo.

BRESAOLA
This air-dried beef from the southern Alps of Italy is served thinly sliced with olive oil. The Italians also cure meats such as wild boar to ensure a year-round supply.

POULTRY

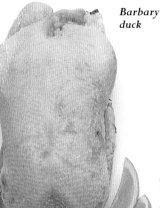

Barbary duck

Quail

Rock Cornish game hen

DUCK

Grown for eggs, meat, and liver, ducks and geese are common in the northern Mediterranean. In southern France they are preserved in their fat to make confit. Barbary ducks are less fatty.

SMALL BIRDS

The inhabitants of the Mediterranean are enthusiastic hunters, and many birds are used in the regional cuisines. Some birds, such as pigeons (squabs) and quail, have grown so popular that they are now farmed. Other wild birds that are regularly consumed include partridge, wood pigeon, woodcock, thrush, and various kinds of wild duck. They are highly valued for their distinctively flavored lean flesh.

POULTRY

The best chickens are free-range and corn-fed, giving their skin a yellow tinge and making their flesh more flavorful. Mediterranean chickens tend to be killed before they grow very large; the young, small Rock Cornish hens are excellent for the grill. Guinea fowl are also widely reared, and turkeys are popular in Italy.

RED MEAT

BEEF

Cattle are difficult to raise in this arid region, although Spain and Italy have popular steak dishes. Beef should be aged with an even color and firm, creamy white fat.

LAMB

Lamb has become the most popular red meat in both the eastern and western Mediterranean diet. Mutton is the meat of sheep over a year old; it is darker and has a more pronounced flavor.

VEAL

This tender meat comes from milk-fed beef calves. It should be light pink in color. For scaloppine, ask your butcher to cut thin slices across the grain and to beat the meat flat.

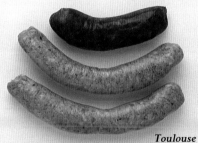

Merguez

Toulouse sausages

VENISON

A fine-textured, dark meat, venison is low in fat and responds well to being marinated before cooking. All game is popular in the Mediterranean — rabbit, hare, and wild boar are also eaten. Some game animals, such as deer, are farmed to ensure a plentiful supply.

OFFAL

Custom and thrift demand that no part of an animal is wasted in the Mediterranean, so offal is often served. The kidneys and livers from lambs and veal calves are especially delicious.

SAUSAGES

Mediterranean sausages have a high meat content and are usually made from pork or lamb. Toulouse sausages and spicy lamb Merguez are specialties.

HERBS AND SPICES

Aromatic spices and scented bunches of fresh herbs are one of the delights of the Mediterranean market. With a few exceptions, most herbs are best used fresh. Spices too can easily lose their pungency and should be kept whole in sealed jars and ground as necessary.

OTHER TYPICAL HERBS & SPICES
caraway seeds, chervil, marjoram
(the cultivated species of oregano),
sage, tarragon

CHIVES
Young chives have a mild onion flavor that complements yogurt- and egg-based dishes.

Nutmeg

DILL
Fresh dill is a fragrant salad herb that imparts a delicately aromatic flavor to many cold egg and yogurt dishes.

BAY LEAVES
Used both fresh and dried, bay has a slightly spicy aroma and is often included in stocks, stews, and marinades. Bay leaves are best dried on the branch.

DRIED MINT
In the eastern Mediterranean, mint is usually dried for cooking. Moroccans make a refreshing tea from bunches of fresh mint.

NUTMEG
Nutmegs should be kept whole and grated when needed. The lacy outer covering of the nutmeg, mace, is also used in sweet and savory dishes.

BLACK PEPPERCORNS
Pepper originally came from the Malabar coast of India and is now the most commonly used spice. It should always be freshly ground.

JUNIPER
Berries from the juniper bush are used in marinades for game. Their scent, reminiscent of the gin in which they are a flavoring, is accentuated by crushing.

CLOVES
The dried flower buds of a tropical evergreen, cloves add a warm, spicy flavor.

CARDAMOM PODS
These seed pods should be crushed to release their full perfumed taste.

FENNEL SEEDS
Toasted fennel seeds have a mild licorice flavor that is delicious with fish.

THYME
A wild herb, thyme grows in many varieties, from creeping plants to bushes. Lemon-scented thyme is particularly flavorful.

Common thyme

Fresh oregano leaves dry well

OREGANO
This popular herb grows wild throughout the Mediterranean. In Greece, rigani, as it is known, is often dried to produce a stronger flavor.

ROSEMARY
A robust, spiky-leaved herb with blue flowers, rosemary has a powerful flavor and is much used by Italian cooks in marinades and with roasted or grilled foods.

BASIL
Fragrant, peppery basil is essential to the cooking of southern France and Italy. It blends beautifully with tomatoes. Avoid the dried version.

CILANTRO
Pungently scented cilantro is important in many North African and Middle Eastern dishes.

Whole sprigs are best for cooking

PARSLEY
Select the sweet, more powerfully flavored, flat-leaved variety, and keep it wrapped in damp newspaper or in a cup of water for freshness.

CINNAMON
Rolled sticks of cinnamon tree bark are used to impart a deep, warm spiciness to meat dishes as well as desserts.

TURMERIC
This vibrant yellow spice is often used to color dishes in place of saffron, but it has a unique, rather bitter flavor.

CUMIN SEEDS
Commonly used in the east and North Africa, cumin seeds are best kept whole and toasted and ground just before using.

SAFFRON
The most expensive spice, saffron is made from the pains-takingly picked stigmas of the Crocus sativus. The best saffron comes from La Mancha in Spain.

ALLSPICE
The warmly aromatic allspice berry is used whole and ground in sweets and savories.

PAPRIKA
Sweet paprika is mildly peppery. It becomes stale quickly, so keep it in a sealed jar.

CORIANDER SEEDS
Coriander seeds have a slight orange scent, quite different from fresh cilantro leaves.

STAPLE FOODS

The Mediterranean diet combines relatively low amounts of meat and fish with beans or grains to provide bulk. Wheat products, such as pasta, couscous, and bread, are especially important; rice is central to both eastern and western Mediterranean cuisine; and high-protein beans are used with flair in a variety of dishes.

OTHER TYPICAL STAPLE FOODS
black-eyed beans; red kidney beans; cannellini beans; butter beans; split peas; semolina; flour

---

GRAINS

COUSCOUS
The staple of the North African countries, couscous is a hard wheat semolina grain. It should be steamed over the spicy broth with which it is traditionally served. Precooked couscous is a useful time-saver.

BULGUR WHEAT
This light, nutty-tasting cereal is made up of boiled cracked grains of wheat. It needs only to be soaked before use and is essential to Lebanese Tabbouleh (see page 130). It may be finely ground or coarse.

POLENTA
A finely ground cornmeal that is popular in northern Italy, polenta is easier to prepare when precooked. It can be served immediately after it is cooked or be allowed to cool, cut into slices, and broiled.

The fragrant grains remain separate after cooking

Valencia rice

Basmati rice

Arborio rice

RICE
It is essential to use the correct rice for a dish, as the various grains differ in texture and flavor. For risotto, use short-grain arborio or vialone rice; for paella, valencia rice; for eastern Mediterranean dishes, long-grain rices, such as basmati and patna, are excellent.

BREADS

UNLEAVENED BREADS
In the eastern Mediterranean, the usual accompaniment to a meal is a flat, unleavened bread. It becomes stale quickly, so several batches a day are made over a fire or in a charcoal oven. Pita bread is common, its "pockets" filled with Falafel (see page 72) for the typical Israeli sandwich.

FOCACCIA
Bakers in the Genoese region of Italy pride themselves on their focaccia, an olive oil bread baked in rectangles and topped with rosemary, coarse salt, and sometimes slivers of onion. It is usually enjoyed as a snack.

Flat bread is popular

Pita

BEANS

BORLOTTI BEANS
Dried borlotti should be soaked overnight and boiled for 10 minutes before simmering. They are much used in Italian soups, cook to a creamy consistency, and have a high protein content.

FAVA BEANS
Dried fava beans have brown skins and white flesh and are especially popular in Egypt, where they are stewed to make Ful Medames (see page 70). They require overnight soaking and long cooking.

CHICKPEAS
Dried chickpeas that have been soaked overnight then boiled have a rich, nutty flavor and texture that is lacking in canned chickpeas. Chickpea flour is used in Nice to make Socca, a popular bread.

Puy lentils *Green lentils*

FLAGEOLETS
Pale green flageolet beans have a delicate flavor and a particular affinity with lamb. They are the dried seeds of a dwarf green bean, much used in France.

WHITE BEANS
Essential for Cassoulet (see page 119), white (Great Northern) beans are used in soups, stews, and salads. Niçois Soupe au Pistou (see page 64) contains fresh white beans.

LENTILS
The best lentils are the tiny dark green ones from Le Puy in France. Both Puy and green lentils generally do not need soaking. They provide an excellent foil to rich meat dishes.

PASTA

Spaghetti

Made from durum wheat flour, dried pasta is a high-carbohydrate food that comes in many shapes; it is important to use the correct shape for a particular sauce. Pasta is not restricted to Italy — various pasta dishes are also found in Spain and the eastern Mediterranean.

Farfalline: tiny shells for soups.

Orecchiette: used to hold sauces.

Cannelloni: tubes for stuffing.

COUNTRY-STYLE BREADS
Few Mediterranean meals are complete without a basket of robust freshly baked bread. Each region, sometimes even each village, has its own distinctive style of bread, using different unrefined flours and distinguished by various flavorings, such as olive oil.

SWEET BREADS
Flavored sweet breads studded with nuts and fruit, and often glazed with honey and sprinkled with seeds, are found especially in the western Mediterranean. Many are associated with religious festivals, as with Greek Easter bread or the Christmas bread of Provence.

Olive oil bread

Walnuts are a popular flavoring

Raisin and nut bread

CHEESE AND YOGURT

The aridity of much of the Mediterranean means that cattle are hard to farm. Only Italy and France boast a wide range of cheeses made from cow's milk. However, cheeses made from sheep's and goat's milk are common, varying from village to village. Yogurt is widely used, both in savory dishes and sweetened with fruit and honey.

OTHER TYPICAL CHEESES

Caciocavallo, semisoft cow's milk cheese (Italy); labneh, made from strained yogurt (Syria and Lebanon); halloumi, sheep's milk cheese (Greece); mascarpone (Italy); Pecorino Romano (Italy); curd cheese

Pyramid-shaped goat cheese

Herb-covered goat cheese

Plain goat cheese

GOAT CHEESES

Goat's milk cheeses may be marinated in olive oil, rolled in ash, leaf-wrapped, or coated with herbs or crushed pepper. They can be round or cylindrical, tiny or vast blocks, pyramids, or squares. The texture may be soft and creamy or hard, depending on maturity. The flavor varies from quite mild to sharp and acidic.

Crottin

MANCHEGO

From the La Mancha region of Spain, famous for saffron and Don Quixote, Manchego is found throughout the country and can be recognized by its distinctive black rind. When mature, it hardens and can be grated; try soft young Manchego with quince paste — Dulce de Membrillo (see page 133).

Thick dark rind

DOLCELATTE

This blue cheese from Italy has a mild flavor and creamy texture. Layered with mascarpone, it is known as Torte di Dolcelatte and makes a very rich after-dinner cheese.

GORGONZOLA

An Italian cheese, Gorgonzola is made in two strengths — mild, or dolce, and strong, or piccante. It cooks well and makes an excellent pasta sauce when mixed with walnuts. Try serving a slice of Gorgonzola with a very ripe pear.

BANON

Cured in Cognac and wrapped in oak leaves, Banon is a distinctive and delicious goat cheese from southwest France. Goat's and sheep's milk cheeses are also wrapped in grape and chestnut leaves.

YOGURT

The most flavorful yogurt is made from sheep's milk. Strained yogurt is good for cooking. Thinned with ice water and sprinkled with herbs, it makes a cooling drink that is popular in the eastern Mediterranean.

Sheep's milk yogurt should be thick and lumpy, with a creamy skin

FETA

Salty feta is the favorite cheese of Greece, forming an essential element of the Greek salad. Feta is made from sheep's milk or goat's milk and is cured in brine. It should be white and crumbly. Feta does not keep well, as it dries out very quickly.

Goat cheese rolled in ash

MOZZARELLA

True mozzarella is made in southern Italy from buffalo milk. Mozzarella made from cow's milk lacks the smooth texture and subtly sour flavor of the original product.

PECORINO SARDO

From Sardinia, this hard sheep's milk cheese can be used like Parmesan, but is slightly more pungent. It is an essential ingredient of Pesto (see page 42).

A tough-rinded cheese

RICOTTA

Italian ricotta is a soft cheese made from the whey extracted from cow's milk. It must be eaten very fresh. Its mild creamy flavor makes it particularly suitable for desserts.

Look for a pale crumbly surface

PARMESAN

Only cheese stamped Parmigiano-Reggiano is the real thing. Always buy Parmesan in blocks, and look for cheese with a grainy quality. Good cheese shops will sell two grades, one for eating as it is and one for grating into dishes.

THE PANTRY

The pantry has always played an important role in the Mediterranean kitchen. The glut of summer produce and the fear of winter scarcity led to a tradition of pickling, preserving, and drying so that cooks could enjoy their favorite ingredients year-round.

ADDITIONAL SUPPLIES
Mostardi di frutti *(fruits pickled in mustard oil)*, coffee, rose water and orange-flower water, sun-dried tomatoes *(a popular antipasto)*, cornichons, salt cod

Cèpe

Chanterelles

Horns of plenty

Bottled pimiento

PICKLES AND PRESERVES

Fruits and vegetables are often preserved for the winter months. Marinated baby artichokes are a delicious antipasto. Bottled red pimiento peppers are much used in Italy and Spain.

DRIED WILD MUSHROOMS

Because of their short season, mushrooms are dried to be reconstituted later in water. Look for chanterelles, cèpes (porcini) and black horns of plenty (trompettes-des-mort).

Artichokes in olive oil

Canned tomatoes

GARLIC

Look for large, firm pink-tinged bulbs, store in a dark place, and discard any that start to sprout. Crushing garlic before chopping enhances its flavor. Roasted bulbs are creamy and sweet.

TOMATO PRODUCTS

Canned plum tomatoes are preferable to underripe hot-house tomatoes. The San Marzano variety is best — avoid those with added seasonings. Tomato paste thickens and enhances flavor.

Tomato paste

TAHINI PASTE

Made from crushed sesame seeds, tahini is much used in the east of the region. It is sold in glass jars and should be kept in a dark cabinet or pantry.

Red hot chili paste

HARISSA

This blend of chilies, oil, and seasonings accompanies couscous.

PICKLED CAPERS

Capers are the buds of a wild shrub. Those pickled in vinegar should be rinsed before use. Salted capers should be soaked.

OLIVE OIL

This essential ingredient varies in flavor and quality. The better the oil, the lower its acidity. Choose a pungent, deep green, extra-virgin cold-pressed oil for dressings and cold dishes, a standard extra-virgin oil for everyday use, a cheaper olive oil for deep-frying, and a herb-scented oil for dressings.

VINEGARS

Wine vinegars and rich, fruity sherry vinegar are much used. Dark, aromatic balsamic vinegar from Modena in Italy is cask-aged and excellent for dressings.

RED WINE

When cooking with wine, try to find one made in the region from which the dish originates. Fortified wines, such as fino sherry and Marsala, are also useful.

Red wine

Balsamic vinegar

Extra-virgin olive oil

White wine vinegar

Olive oil infused with thyme

Green olives marinated with lemon and spices

Niçoise olives

OLIVES

Tiny black niçoise olives and marinated green cracked olives are much used in cooking and as an antipasto or snack. Pitted olives are usually inferior in flavor to those with the pit.

HONEY

The traditional sweetener of ancient Greek and Roman civilizations, honey is used in savory and sweet dishes. Look for honeys scented with a particular herb or flower, such as lavender.

Coarse flakes can be ground as necessary

ANCHOVIES

Most anchovies are packed in olive oil, but some of the best are packed in salt and should be rinsed well before use. They are particularly widely used in Provençal and Italian cooking.

SEA SALT

This salt has a unique flavor, derived from the different salts in the sea water evaporated to produce it.

CLASSIC
DISHES

*The Mediterranean boasts hundreds of classic dishes,
the recipes for which are handed down through
generations of families. The dishes chosen here, from the
sumptuous Italian Zuppa di Pesce to the little meze
dishes of Turkey and Greece, particularly characterize
the region's cooking and should give you a taste for
discovering many more traditional specialties.
All the dishes serve 4, unless otherwise indicated.*

ZUPPA DI PESCE

Italian fish soup

All over the Mediterranean, fish soups are made from the day's catch. Each region, indeed each fishing village, has its own variation. This Italian version is more of a stew than a soup. With its tomatoes, wine, olive oil, garlic, and delicious fish and shellfish, it epitomizes for me the flavors of the Mediterranean.

INGREDIENTS

3lb (1.5kg) fish (at least 3 of the following: sea bream, red or gray mullet, fresh sardines, mackerel, monkfish, sea bass, sole)
4 garlic cloves
1½lb (750g) ripe plum tomatoes, peeled and seeded
3 tbsp chopped fresh parsley
1½ cups (350ml) dry white wine
½lb (250g) small fresh squid
1lb (500g) mussels and/or small clams
⅓ cup (75ml) olive oil
1 onion, chopped
2 dried red chilies, chopped
salt and black pepper
¼ tsp saffron
4 scallops
8 large cooked shrimp

PREPARATION

1 Remove the fish heads. Place them in a pan with a whole garlic clove, one fourth of the tomatoes, a teaspoon of parsley, one third of the wine, and 6 cups of water. Bring to a boil. Simmer for 30 minutes. Strain the resulting stock.
2 Prepare the squid and clean the mussels and clams (see page 153). Cut any fish longer than 6in (15cm) into 3in (7cm) pieces. Chop the remaining garlic and coarsely chop the rest of the tomatoes.
3 Warm the oil in a large pot. Cook the onion until soft, about 20 minutes. Add the garlic and two thirds of the remaining parsley. Cook for 10 minutes.
4 Add the tomatoes and chilies. Cook for 10 minutes longer, stirring frequently, until the tomatoes have broken down. Pour in the rest of the wine, turn up the heat, bring to a boil, and allow to bubble for 2 minutes. Add the stock, plenty of seasoning, and the saffron. Bring to a boil. Reduce the heat and simmer, uncovered, for 15 minutes.
5 Add the fish in order of cooking time: squid, firm fish, whole fish, scallops, shrimp, and, finally, mussels and clams. The total cooking time should not exceed 20 minutes.
6 Sprinkle with parsley and serve.

Clams

Dry white wine

Parsley

Tomatoes

Garlic

Scallops

Squid

Sea bream

Fresh sardines

Red mullet

Onion

Red chilies

Salt

Black pepper

Saffron

Shrimp

Olive oil

Mussels

GAZPACHO ANDALUZ

Chilled Andalusian gazpacho

This soup is essentially a puréed salad, with the refreshing characteristics that description suggests. Spain boasts many different kinds of gazpacho, including an elegant white almond soup, Ajo Blanco con Uvas (see page 60), inherited from the Moors. The soup below is the classic, tomato-rich version – the juicier and riper the tomatoes, the better it will taste.

INGREDIENTS

2lb (1kg) very ripe plum tomatoes, peeled, and seeded
2 green peppers, peeled, cored, and seeded
1 cucumber, peeled
3 slices white bread
½ red onion, chopped
2 garlic cloves, chopped
⅓ cup (80ml) extra-virgin olive oil
2 tbsp sherry vinegar
salt
1 cup (250ml) ice water

GARNISHES

2 tomatoes
1 green pepper, peeled, cored, and seeded
½ cucumber
1 red onion
2 hard-boiled eggs, peeled
2 slices white bread, crusts removed
olive oil for frying

PREPARATION

1 Chop the tomatoes coarsely, reserving the juice. Dice the green peppers. Chop the cucumber. Trim the bread crusts and tear the bread into small squares.

2 Put the tomatoes and their juice, the peppers, cucumber, onion, garlic, bread, oil, and vinegar with some salt and the ice water in a food processor. Blend until well mixed, but not too smooth – the soup should have texture.

3 Check the balance of oil and vinegar, adding more of each if necessary. Chill the soup for a minimum of 2 hours.

4 Prepare the garnishes. Dice all the vegetables and chop the hard-boiled eggs. Cut the bread into small cubes and fry the cubes in olive oil until they turn golden brown on both sides. Arrange the garnishes in small bowls.

5 If desired, thin the soup with more ice water before serving (though it should remain fairly thick). Serve, passing the garnishes separately.

Red onion

White bread

Cucumber

Green peppers

Tomatoes

Garlic

Olive oil

Sherry vinegar

Salt

Hard-boiled
eggs

TAPAS

Tapas, meaning "covers" or "lids," take their name from the little plates of simple appetizers traditionally placed over your glass in a Spanish bar. This selection of some of the slightly more elaborate tapas dishes would be ideal for entertaining.

CHAMPIÑONES AL AJILLO

Mushrooms in garlic

This is the favorite way to prepare mushrooms and works well with cultivated or wild varieties. The mushrooms are sautéed in garlicky olive oil, sprinkled with fresh parsley, and finished with a squeeze of lemon.
See page 85 for recipe.

ESPINACAS A LA CATALANA

Spinach Catalan style

The natural sweetness of young spinach is accentuated in this rich dish by pine nuts and plump raisins.
See page 80 for recipe.

PINCHOS MORUNOS

Pork kebabs

These little kebabs are named after the Moorish invaders who first brought spices to Spain. Today these kebabs are traditionally made with pork.
See page 107 for recipe.

Salpicon de Mariscos

Shellfish salad

*The key to this dish is the piquant sauce,
spiked with capers and cornichons,
in which the shrimp and mussels are
marinated. You can include other
shellfish such as clams or periwinkles,
or branch out with squid, but do not
be tempted to put in the more delicate
lobster or crab.*

See page 91 for recipe.

Habas con Jamon

Fava beans with ham

*The air-dried ham of Spain rivals in
quality its more famous Italian cousin
from Parma. It has few better partners
than tiny juicy fava beans. The beans
are cooked without water, reflecting the
fact that in parts of Spain water is more
precious than olive oil.*

See page 80 for recipe.

Tortilla

Potato omelet

*Nothing like the French omelet, the
tortilla is a thick wedge of eggs and
potatoes, at its best when served warm
or cold rather than straight from the
pan. No tapas bar is complete without
tortilla, which is also ideal picnic food.*

See page 85 for recipe.

IMAM BAYILDI

Turkish stuffed eggplant

The Imam swooned when he ate this dish, so the story goes in Turkey, because he found it so delicious. Less romantic historians have suggested he was overcome by the amount of olive oil used in the preparation — but if the oil is hot enough, the eggplants will absorb very little of it as they fry. I know which explanation I prefer.

INGREDIENTS

4 medium eggplants
salt
2 green peppers, cored and seeded
1 large onion
1lb (500g) plum tomatoes, peeled and seeded
1¾ cups (400ml) olive oil
3 garlic cloves, chopped
1 tbsp tomato paste
1 tsp sweet paprika
1 tsp ground allspice
½ tsp black pepper
3 tbsp chopped fresh parsley

PREPARATION

1 Wash the eggplants, leaving the stems intact. With a sharp knife, make a 2in (5cm) deep slit from the stalk to the base, being careful not to cut through completely. Sprinkle salt into the slits and set aside for 20 minutes.

2 Cut the peppers into fine strips. Peel the onion, cut in half, and slice into fine half-moons. Chop the tomatoes into small pieces.

3 Heat one fourth of the oil in a large frying pan over medium heat. Add the peppers, onion, and garlic and fry for 20 minutes, stirring frequently.

4 Preheat the oven to 375°F (190°C).

5 Add the tomatoes, tomato paste, spices, and half the parsley to the onion and pepper mixture. Cook for 10 minutes longer, stirring frequently.

6 Rinse the eggplants and pat dry. Heat the remaining olive oil and fry the eggplants for 10 minutes, turning several times. Remove and drain on paper towels.

7 Place the eggplants slit side up in an earthenware dish in which they will fit snugly. Carefully open the slits and pile in the onion, pepper, and tomato mixture. Pour enough boiling water into the dish to come halfway up the sides of the eggplants.

8 Bake in the oven for 45 minutes, until very tender. Allow the eggplants to cool in the liquid, then lift out with a slotted spoon. Sprinkle with the remaining parsley and serve.

Tomatoes

Onion

Green peppers

Salt

Eggplants

Olive oil

Garlic

Tomato paste

Sweet paprika

Ground allspice

Black pepper

Parsley

GNOCCHI AL PESTO

Italian potato dumplings with pesto sauce

The classic Italian pesto combines well with many kinds of pasta, particularly *trenette*, but in the original Genoese dish it is traditionally served with potato gnocchi. These little white dumplings are surprisingly light, and the perfect foil to luscious green basil-scented pesto.

INGREDIENTS

GNOCCHI
1½lb (750g) medium-size red potatoes
good pinch of salt
1½ cups (175g) all-purpose flour, plus flour to dust
PESTO
1 large garlic clove
½ tsp salt
2 cups (60g) fresh basil
⅓ cup (30g) freshly grated Pecorino Sardo
⅔ cup (60g) freshly grated Parmesan
1¼ cups (45g) pine nuts
⅔ cup (150ml) extra-virgin olive oil

PREPARATION

1 To make the gnocchi, boil the potatoes in their skins for 30 minutes or until tender (do not prick to test). Drain, peel, then mash with the salt.
2 Sift the flour then, with your hands, lightly work it into the mashed potato, a tablespoon at a time, until you have a smooth dough.
3 Split the dough in half. Lay one half on a floured surface. Using your palms, roll it out into a long sausage shape. Cut the sausage in half and roll out each half again, until it is about the thickness of your thumb. Repeat with the remaining dough.
4 Flour two baking sheets. Cut the dough at ¾in (2cm) intervals. Take a fork and, holding the curved tip toward you, press each piece of dough against the prongs. The gnocchi should be curved, with an indent on one side and ridges on the other to pick up the sauce. Lay them on the trays.
5 To make the pesto, crush the garlic with the salt (see page 150). Tear the basil and, using a mortar and pestle or food processor, combine it with the garlic and salt. Add the cheeses and pine nuts and briefly grind again.
6 Add the oil in a steady trickle, stirring continually or keeping the food processor on, until well blended.
7 Bring a pan of salted water to a boil. Cook the gnocchi in batches – they are done as soon as they rise to the surface (1–2 minutes). Remove with a slotted spoon and place in a warm serving dish. Spoon over the pesto and serve immediately.

Basil

Garlic

Flour

Salt

Potatoes

Parmesan

Pine nuts

Olive oil

Pecorino
Sardo

MEZE

As *tapas* are a way of life in Spain, so are *meze* in the eastern Mediterranean. Here there always seems to be time to enjoy a cup of coffee or a drink with a few little savory pastries and a selection of freshly made dips. Like tapas, meze make perfect party food.

BABA GHANOUJ

Purée of broiled eggplant

Eggplants broiled until their flesh blackens acquire a new sweetness. In this famous Lebanese dish, the flesh is then mixed with tahini paste and spiked with lemon juice. You can leave out the tahini if you like — then the dish is known as "poor man's caviar."
See page 70 for recipe.

HUMMUS BI TAHINI

Chickpea and sesame dip

It is hard to imagine a meze table without a plate of hummus, puréed chickpeas garnished with spicy red oil and parsley, and served with warm flat bread.
See page 70 for recipe.

TSATSIKI

Yogurt and cucumber dip

When the midday sun blazes down, nothing can be more appetizing than a dish of chilled tsatsiki. Use fresh bread to scoop up this refreshing yogurt dip.
See page 70 for recipe.

BÖREKS

Stuffed savory pastries

Although the little pastries known in Turkey as böreks are traditionally made with wet pastry, a much more practical alternative is to use ready-made frozen phyllo pastry. Feta cheese crumbled and mixed with chopped dill makes a deliciously simple filling.
See page 72 for recipe.

FALAFEL

Chickpea fritters

Falafel is the favorite street food of Israel, where they are made with chickpeas (as opposed to the dried fava beans used in Egypt). They are at their very best straight from the pan. For a more complete snack, sandwich falafel in a pita pocket and top with hummus.
See page 72 for recipe.

DOLMATHES

Stuffed grape leaves

Mediterranean cooks make use of all available ingredients. The vine may be grown to provide wine, but its leaves are not allowed to go to waste. Stuffed with a savory rice mixture, they become delectable morsels in their own right.
See page 72 for recipe.

DJEJ EMSHMEL

Tagine of chicken with lemons and olives

Moroccan cuisine is famous for its tagines, delicately spiced casseroles that owe their name to the earthenware pot with its chimney-shaped lid in which they are cooked. This recipe for chicken gently simmered with fat juicy olives and preserved lemons is one of my favorites. Bread is the traditional accompaniment, but Roz bi Saffran (see page 130) complements it perfectly.

Saffron

Ground cumin

Ground cinnamon

Ground ginger

Black pepper

Garlic

Onion

INGREDIENTS

6oz (175g) green cracked olives
1 chicken, about 3½lb (1.75kg)
1 onion
3 garlic cloves, finely chopped
1 tsp black pepper
1 tsp ground ginger
½ tsp ground cinnamon
½ tsp ground cumin
good pinch of saffron
salt
¼ cup (60ml) olive oil
1 large bunch each of fresh parsley and cilantro
2 preserved lemons (see page 133) or 1 fresh lemon
juice of 1 fresh lemon

PREPARATION

1 Cover the olives with water and let soak for an hour, changing the water after 30 minutes.
2 Remove any excess fat from the cavity of the chicken, then place it in an oval casserole dish.
3 Grate the flesh of the onion, making sure you catch the juices, and add to the casserole with the garlic, spices, a pinch of salt, and the oil.
4 Wash the herbs and set aside enough from each bunch to produce 1 tablespoon of chopped leaves. Tie the remainder in a bunch and add to the dish.
5 Pour in just enough water to cover the chicken. Bring to a boil. Reduce the heat and simmer for 30 minutes, turning the chicken after 15 minutes.
6 Drain and rinse the olives. Quarter the preserved lemons and rinse well (or quarter 1 fresh lemon). Add to the dish, together with the olives and lemon juice. Cover and cook 20 minutes longer.
7 Remove the chicken and wrap in foil. Turn up the heat under the dish and boil rapidly until the sauce is reduced by half. Remove the bunch of herbs and add the fresh chopped leaves. Check the seasoning, adding more salt or lemon juice if desired.
8 Cut the chicken into portions and spoon over the spicy sauce. Serve with warm flat bread or fragrant Roz bi Saffran.

Green cracked olives

Chicken

Salt

Olive oil

Parsley

Cilantro

Preserved lemons

Fresh lemon
and juice

PISSALADIERE

Provençal onion tart

The classic *pissaladière* is a round bread tart, deeply filled with the delectably sweet onions of the region. This favorite dish from Nice derives its name from the *pissala*, or salt fish paste, with which it was originally smeared. Today it is usually topped with anchovies and olives.

INGREDIENTS

DOUGH
2½ cups (300g) unbleached all-purpose flour,
plus flour to dust
1 tsp salt
1 tsp sugar
1 tbsp active dry yeast
1 large egg, beaten
2 tbsp olive oil

FILLING
3lb (1.5kg) sweet white onions
2 garlic cloves, peeled and lightly crushed
but kept whole
½ tsp salt
3 tbsp olive oil
bouquet garni made up of 1 fresh bay leaf and
2 sprigs each of fresh thyme and rosemary
8 anchovy fillets in olive oil
16 small black olives, preferably niçoise

PREPARATION

1 Combine the flour and salt in an ovenproof bowl. Place in a very low oven for 10 minutes.

2 Mix the sugar into ⅔ cup (150ml) warm water, then whisk in the yeast. Cover and leave for 10 minutes, until frothy.

3 Make a well in the center of the flour. Pour in the egg, oil, and yeast mixture. Stir with a wooden spoon, then work the dough with floured hands. The mixture will be sticky at first but, after a few minutes, it will become smooth. Work 5 minutes longer, until pliable.

4 Sprinkle the dough with a little flour. Cover with a damp cloth and leave in a warm place for 1 hour, or until doubled in size (see page 151).

5 Meanwhile, make the filling. Peel the onions, cut in half, and slice into fine half-moons. Place in a heavy-lidded pan with the garlic, salt, 1 tbsp of oil, and the bouquet garni. Cook, covered, over low heat for 1 hour, stirring occasionally. The onion should become very soft but should not brown.

6 Preheat the oven to 350°F (180°C). Oil a 10in (25cm) tart pan. Punch down the dough (see page 151) and press it out with your hands to fill the pan.

Flour

Salt

Sugar

Active dry yeast

Egg

Bake in the preheated oven for 10 minutes to dry out the dough. Remove the pan, then turn the oven to 450°F (230°C).

7 Fill the dough case with the onion, discarding the bouquet garni and garlic. Arrange the anchovies in a lattice over the top of the onion and scatter the olives in between. Pour the remaining oil over the tart. Bake for 15 minutes and serve warm.

Olive oil

Niçoise olives

Sweet white
onions

Anchovies

Garlic

Bouquet garni

49

GRILLED FOOD

Throughout the Mediterranean, whether on the shady terrace of a villa or at a street stall, you will find people grilling food over charcoal. It may be meat, fish, or vegetables, frequently marinated with a few spices and herbs, and the results are served simply, with bread and perhaps a little freshly made sauce.

Rock salt

DJEJ MESHWI

Grilled spring chicken

In the eastern Mediterranean, there are restaurants devoted to serving nothing but spring chickens grilled over charcoal. For me, nothing can be more mouth-watering than the sight and smell of these little marinated chickens rotating on the spit.
See page 106 for recipe.

ŞIŞ KÖFTESI

Ground meat on skewers

These skewered ground meat kebabs can fairly be called the hamburger of the eastern Mediterranean. Although they are usually made with lamb, beef can be used if it is not too lean (the fat provides flavor.)
See page 106 for recipe.

KILIÇ SISTE TARATOR

Swordfish kebabs with walnut sauce

This dish is the pride of the myriad restaurants that line the Bosporus outside Istanbul. The kebabs of swordfish interspersed with bay leaves sizzle away while you sip your drink and look at the lights of the city across the water.
See page 92 for recipe.

Tarator sauce

PESCE ALLA GRIGLIA SALSA VERDE

Grilled fish with green sauce

Salsa verde, or "green sauce," is deliciously piquant and, being uncooked, very simple to make. In Italy it is traditionally served with boiled meats, but it also makes a perfect accompaniment to grilled fish.
See page 96 for recipe.

Salsa Verde

ŞIŞ KEBAB

Lamb kebabs

This classically simple dish is found all over the eastern Mediterranean. Chunks of lamb are marinated in olive oil and lemon juice and cooked over charcoal for added flavor.
See page 107 for recipe.

PAELLA VALENCIANA

Valencian paella

Taking its name from the *paellera*, the large two-handled shallow pan in which it is prepared, this famous rice dish is traditionally cooked over a wood fire. The people of the Albufera Lake region in Valencia claim to have invented the dish, and the original paella once included rabbit, snails, and eels, as well as the flat beans for which the area is famous. Today there are many variants of paella – this is one of my favorites. Serves 8.

INGREDIENTS

20 small clams
½ lb (250g) long beans, such as runner or flat, trimmed
6oz (175g) plum tomatoes, peeled and seeded
salt
1 chicken, about 3lb (1.5kg), cut up into 16 pieces (see page 154)
½ lb (250g) cooking chorizo
½ cup (125ml) olive oil
¼ lb (125g) fresh peas, shelled
2 garlic cloves, finely chopped
1 sprig fresh rosemary
5 cups (1.4 liters) chicken stock (see page 155)
¼ tsp saffron
3½ cups (500g) valencia or other short-grain rice, such as arborio
2 lemons, quartered

PREPARATION

1 Clean the clams (see page 153). Cut the beans into 1½in (3.5cm) pieces. Chop the tomatoes coarsely, being careful not to lose the juices.
2 Sprinkle salt over the chicken pieces. Cut the chorizo into 1in (2.5cm) slices.
3 Heat the oil in a large, deep round pan, preferably a paellera or a two-handled pan. The pan should not be too heavy. Add the chicken and the chorizo and cook for 5 minutes, turning the pieces from time to time until they are browned on all sides.
4 Add the beans, peas, chopped tomatoes, garlic, rosemary, and chicken stock. Bring to a boil, then stir in the saffron. Cover and leave to simmer for approximately 10 minutes.
5 Add the rice and salt to taste. Quickly stir all the ingredients together and bring back to a boil. Lower heat, cover, and simmer for 10 minutes.
6 Remove the lid and add the clams. Cover and cook for 10 minutes longer, until the rice has absorbed all the liquid.
7 Take the pan off the heat, cover it with a clean dry dish towel, and let stand for 10 minutes before serving with lemon quarters.

Chorizo

Salt

Tomatoes

Runner beans

Clams

Chicken

Olive oil

Peas

Garlic

Rosemary

Chicken stock

Saffron

Valencia rice

Lemons

KOUNELLI STIFATHO

Greek rabbit casserole

The ancient Greeks liked to use honey and vinegar to give a sweet and sour touch to their cooking, a habit preserved in this hunters' casserole. Traditionally, rabbit or hare is used, but beef also works well. Whichever meat you choose, the real delight of the dish is the rich, spicy sauce studded with baby onions and scented with mountain herbs.

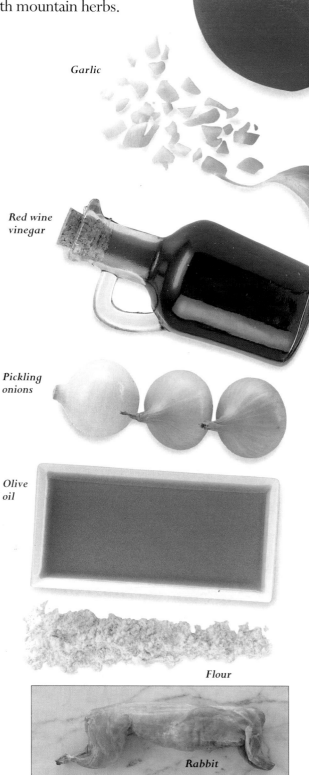

Garlic

Red wine vinegar

Pickling onions

Olive oil

Flour

Rabbit

INGREDIENTS

1 large rabbit, about 3lb (1.5kg), cut up into 8 pieces
flour, to dust
⅔ cup (150ml) olive oil
2lb (1kg) small onions
½ cup (125ml) red wine vinegar
3 garlic cloves, chopped
1lb (500g) plum tomatoes, peeled
1 tbsp ground cumin
1 cinnamon stick
8 whole allspice
8 cloves
1 tbsp clear honey
½ cup (125g) tomato paste
2½ cups (600ml) robust red wine
salt and black pepper
bouquet garni made up of 2 fresh bay leaves, zest of 1 orange, 3 sprigs each of fresh thyme and oregano

PREPARATION

1 Preheat the oven to 350°F (180°C).

2 Dust the rabbit pieces with flour.

3 Heat half the oil in a large heavy frying pan. Add the rabbit pieces and sauté for 5 minutes to brown them. Transfer to an earthenware casserole.

4 Plunge the onions into boiling water to loosen the skins, remove with a slotted spoon, and peel.

5 Turn the heat to low and add the onions to the pan. Cook for 20 minutes, turning the onions until they are brown all over. Transfer to the casserole.

6 Drain the excess oil from the pan. Turn the heat to medium and add the vinegar and garlic. Cook for 2 minutes, stirring with a wooden spoon.

7 Add the tomatoes, spices, and honey to the pan. Cook for 5 minutes, then stir in the tomato paste, red wine, and remaining oil. Bring to a boil, season generously, and pour into the casserole.

8 Tuck the bouquet garni into the casserole, leaving the string outside for easy removal.

9 Cover the casserole and place in the oven. Bake for 30 minutes. Reduce the heat to 300°F (150°C), and bake for 1½ hours. Check the seasoning, remove the bouquet garni and cinnamon, and serve.

Cloves

Whole
allspice

Clear
honey

Tomato
paste

Red wine

Salt

Black
pepper

Bouquet
garni

Cinnamon
stick

Ground
cumin

Tomatoes

ROUGETS A LA NIÇOISE

Red mullet Niçois style

For me, red mullet are the quintessential fish of the Mediterranean. On my honeymoon in Turkey, spent aboard a little fishing boat, we bought some straight from the fishermen and fried them there and then in olive oil. That remains a most delicious memory. This equally simple but delectable dish from Nice uses just about every classic ingredient of the region.

INGREDIENTS

8 small red mullet, weighing 6–8oz (175–250g) each
or 4 large red mullet or red snapper, weighing
12–14oz (375–425g) each
½ cup (125ml) olive oil
1 onion, finely chopped
3 garlic cloves, finely chopped
3 tbsp chopped fresh parsley
1 tsp tomato paste
¼ cup (60ml) dry white wine
2lb (1kg) tomatoes, peeled and chopped
salt and black pepper
flour, to dust
1 cup small black olives, preferably niçoise
¼ cup capers, rinsed and drained
16 anchovy fillets in olive oil
2 lemons, sliced

PREPARATION

1 Scale and gut the mullet (see page 152). If you like a slightly gamey flavor, leave in the liver (as is traditional in Nice).
2 Preheat the oven to 350°F (180°C).
3 Heat 4 tbsp of oil and fry the onion over medium heat, stirring frequently, until golden. Add the garlic and almost all the parsley, reserving a little for a garnish, and fry for another 5 minutes.
4 Stir the tomato paste into the white wine. Add the tomatoes, tomato paste and wine mixture, and seasoning to the pan. Simmer uncovered for 15 minutes, stirring occasionally to help the tomatoes break down, until you have a thick tomato sauce.
5 Season the flour and lightly dust the mullet. Warm the remaining oil in a nonstick skillet in which the fish will lie flat. When the oil is very hot, add the fish. Fry for 4 minutes on each side, then remove with a slotted spoon.
6 Arrange the mullet in a single layer in an earthenware dish, and pour over the sauce. Arrange the olives, capers, anchovies, and the lemon slices over the top. Place in the preheated oven and bake for 15 minutes. Serve hot, straight from the dish.

White wine

Tomato paste

Parsley

Garlic

Onion

Olive oil

Red mullet

Tomatoes

Salt

Black
pepper

Flour

Niçoise
olives

Capers

Anchovies

Lemons

RECIPES

The countries around the Mediterranean Sea may follow the same basic principles in the kitchen, but they also offer a wealth of regional variety. This recipe collection reflects that rich diversity. Here you will find a delicate chilled white soup from Andalusia and a warming minestrone from Livorno, a spicy tagine from Fez, an herb-scented Provençal daube, and sardines grilled Turkish style. A tempting menu planner will also help you assemble memorable meals, from a leisurely lunch for a summer's day to a delicately spiced North African feast. All the dishes serve 4, unless otherwise indicated.

SOUPS

Mediterranean food has its roots in a peasant culture, and soups are the ultimate peasant fare. Several of those featured here are substantial enough to serve as main courses. Try a real Minestrone, so thick you can stand your spoon up in it, the fragrant basil-scented Soupe au Pistou of Provence, or Harira, the spicy Moroccan soup traditionally served as dusk falls during Ramadan. For hotter days, look to the lighter, elegant chilled soups, such as the garlicky white version of gazpacho found in Andalusia or the simple cucumber and yogurt soup of Turkey.

AJO BLANCO CON UVAS

Iced almond soup with grapes

Known as "white gazpacho," this soup is believed to have been introduced to Andalusia by the Moors, who certainly brought the almond trees that yield the central ingredient. The thick, garlicky white soup, studded with grapes, should be served very cold.

INGREDIENTS

½ cup (125g) blanched almonds, coarsely chopped
3 garlic cloves
½ tsp salt
4 slices slightly stale white bread, crusts removed
½lb (250g) seedless white grapes
⅓ cup (90ml) extra-virgin olive oil
2 tbsp white vinegar
3½ cups (900ml) ice water

PREPARATION

1 Grind the chopped almonds, garlic, and salt to a fine paste. (Traditionally this stage is done with a mortar and pestle, but a food processor can also be used successfully.)
2 Soak the bread for 5 minutes in a little cold water, then squeeze it dry. Add the bread to the almond and garlic paste, then grind or process again until smooth.
3 Pour boiling water over the grapes to loosen the skins, then drain and peel them.
4 Very slowly beat the oil into the almond, garlic, and bread paste, followed by the vinegar.
5 Pour in the ice water, check for salt, and place the soup in the refrigerator to chill thoroughly.
6 Just before serving, garnish the chilled soup with the peeled grapes.

ÇAÇIK SOUPA

Cold soup of yogurt and cucumber

Çaçik (or tsatsiki, as it is known in Greece), the traditional Turkish meze of yogurt and cucumber, can also be served in soup form when thinned with ice water. Studded with pale green cucumber and flecked with bright green dill, this soup makes a refreshing appetizer on a hot day.

INGREDIENTS

1½ cucumbers, peeled
salt
4 cups (750ml) plain yogurt, strained through cheesecloth
juice of ½ lemon
2 tbsp olive oil
½ garlic clove, minced
1 cup (250ml) ice water
4 tbsp finely chopped fresh dill

PREPARATION

1 Coarsely grate the cucumbers, using a food processor or grater. Place in a bowl, sprinkle well with salt, and let stand for 15 minutes.
2 Beat the yogurt with the lemon juice, oil, garlic, and ice water. If necessary, add a little more water to thin the mixture, but the finished soup should be quite thick.
3 Rinse the cucumber, pat dry with paper towels, and add to the yogurt. Stir in the dill, reserving a little for garnish. Chill well, and garnish with the remaining dill before serving.

VARIATION

• Use a mixture of half fresh dill and half fresh mint to flavor the soup, and replace one cup of the yogurt with sour cream.

SOUPE DE POTIRON

Pumpkin soup

This rich yellow soup from Provence is enormously comforting on a cool evening. Choose small sweet pumpkins rather than overgrown ones, which are best kept for Halloween. Serves 6–8.

INGREDIENTS

3½lb (1.75kg) pumpkin
3 white onions
1 garlic clove, finely chopped
2 fresh sage leaves or pinch dried sage
2 tbsp olive oil
salt and black pepper
⅓ cup (90g) long-grain rice, rinsed and drained
shavings of fresh Parmesan, to serve

PREPARATION

1 Peel the pumpkin and cut the flesh into 1in (2.5cm) cubes. Peel the onions, cut in half, and slice into fine half-moons.
2 Place the pumpkin, onion, and garlic in a large heavy pan with the sage and oil. Pour over 10 cups (2.5 liters) of boiling water. Add seasoning to taste, and simmer slowly for 45 minutes.
3 Purée the soup with a blender or food processor.
4 Return the soup to the pan, and bring back to a boil. Add the rice, and cook for 15 minutes, until soft. Check the seasoning, then garnish with a few shavings of Parmesan.

VARIATION

• Replace the rice with ⅓ cup (90g) vermicelli, broken up and cooked in the soup for 10 minutes.

MINESTRONE ALLA LIVORNESE

Vegetable soup Livorno style

There is no definitive recipe for minestrone, or "big soup" as it is translated. Each region, each village, each family in Italy has its own recipe and varies the vegetables according to the season. This is a cold-weather version from Livorno. Serves 6–8.

INGREDIENTS

¼lb (125g) pancetta, diced
2 onions, finely chopped
2 garlic cloves, finely chopped
2 tbsp extra-virgin olive oil
1lb (500g) plum tomatoes, peeled, seeded, and chopped
¼lb (125g) prosciutto, cut into strips
bouquet garni made up of 1 fresh bay leaf and 2 sprigs each of fresh parsley, thyme, and rosemary
¾ cup (125g) dried borlotti or pinto beans, soaked overnight
3lb (1.5kg) mixed vegetables, such as carrots, cauliflower, savoy cabbage, leeks, celery, potatoes, pumpkin
salt and black pepper
extra-virgin olive oil and freshly grated Parmesan, to serve

PREPARATION

1 Place a large heavy pan over medium heat. Put the pancetta, onion, garlic, and olive oil in the pan and cook for 10 minutes, stirring frequently.
2 Add the tomatoes and cook for 5 minutes longer, until they have broken down.
3 Stir in the prosciutto, the bouquet garni, the beans, and 8 cups (2 liters) of water and bring to a boil. Reduce to a simmer, cover, and cook for 1 hour, or until the beans are tender.
4 Meanwhile, prepare the vegetables, peeling and dicing where necessary, cutting cabbage into thin strips, and leeks into thin slices.
5 After the soup has cooked for 1 hour, add the vegetables. Check for saltiness, and season. Let simmer gently for 30 minutes longer, or until the vegetables are tender. Discard the bouquet garni.
6 Serve the minestrone with a little pitcher of extra-virgin olive oil and plenty of grated Parmesan.

VARIATIONS

• Add ½ cup (90g) *tubetti*, or other small pasta, 15 minutes before the end of cooking time.
• Make a summery Genoese green minestrone, with leeks, green beans, Swiss chard, zucchini, and cannellini beans. Garnish with basil leaves or with a tablespoon of freshly made Pesto (see page 42).

Bouquet garni

Prosciutto

Tomatoes

Olive oil

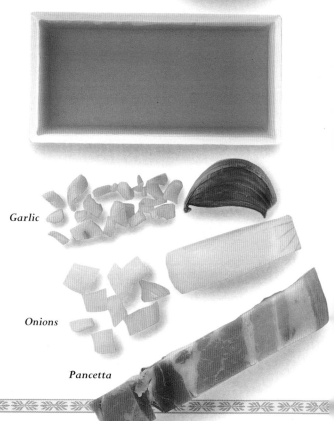

Garlic

Onions

Pancetta

Dried borlotti
beans

Carrots

Cauliflower

Savoy
cabbage

Leeks

Salt

Black
pepper

Parmesan

SOUPE AU PISTOU

Vegetable soup with pistou sauce

*Genoa has pesto, Nice has pistou, without the pine
nuts. In the early summer months, both cities
prepare a delectable green vegetable soup, finished
with their own famous sauce.*

INGREDIENTS

2 young leeks
⅓ cup (90ml) olive oil
6 garlic cloves
12oz (375g) plum tomatoes, peeled, seeded, and chopped
½lb (250g) small zucchini
½lb (250g) thin green beans
6oz (175g) Swiss chard tops, thoroughly washed
salt and black pepper
*bouquet garni made up of 2 sprigs each of
fresh parsley, sage, and basil*
½lb (250g) fresh fava beans, shelled and peeled
3oz (90g) vermicelli
2 cups (60g) fresh basil leaves, torn
½ cup (60g) freshly grated Parmesan

PREPARATION

1 Remove the green ends of the leeks and finely
chop the white parts. Heat 2 tbsp of oil in a heavy
pan over low heat and add the leeks and
2 garlic cloves, finely chopped. Cook for
10 minutes, until softened, then add the tomatoes.
Cook gently for 5 minutes longer, until the
tomatoes have broken down.
2 Meanwhile, dice the zucchini and cut the green
beans into 1in (2.5cm) lengths. Cut the Swiss
chard tops into strips. When the tomatoes have
broken down, add these vegetables to the pan,
together with 8 cups (2 liters) of boiling water,
some seasoning, and the bouquet garni. Bring back
to a boil and simmer for 25 minutes.
3 Add the fava beans and vermicelli to the pan and
let cook for 10–15 minutes.
4 Prepare the pistou. First pound the remaining
garlic with a pinch of salt (this should be done with
a mortar and pestle for best results). When the
garlic has become a paste, add the basil leaves.
Pound again until you have a smooth green paste,
then, using a fork, incorporate the Parmesan.
Finally, stir in the remaining olive oil.
5 Remove the soup from the heat and correct the
seasoning. Discard the bouquet garni. Stir in the
pistou just before serving. (Once the pistou has
been added, do not reheat the soup.)

HARIRA

Ramadan soup

*Each night of the Muslim month of Ramadan
in Morocco, steaming cauldrons of harira await the
faithful. The spicy, herb-laden soup rewards those
who have fasted during the long daylight hours.
This dish serves 6–8.*

INGREDIENTS

¾ cup (175g) dried chickpeas, soaked overnight
1 chicken carcass or 1lb (500g) lamb bones
*1 large bunch fresh cilantro, plus 3 tbsp
chopped fresh cilantro*
*1 large bunch fresh parsley, plus 3 tbsp
chopped fresh parsley*
½ cup (125g) yellow lentils
1 tsp turmeric
2 tsp ground cinnamon
1 tsp ground ginger
1 tsp ground cumin
1 tsp black pepper
salt
2 mild white onions
1lb (500g) plum tomatoes, peeled, seeded, and chopped
1 tsp tomato paste
2 tbsp all-purpose flour
2 tbsp olive oil
juice of 1 lemon
1 whole lemon, cut into wedges,
6–8 tsp harissa, to serve (see page 30)

PREPARATION

1 Drain the chickpeas and put them in a large pan
with the chicken carcass, the bunches of herbs tied
together and 10 cups (2.5 liters) of water. Bring to
a boil, cover, and simmer for 1 hour, or until the
chickpeas are soft. Remove the chicken carcass and
the bunches of herbs and discard.
2 Add the lentils, spices, and salt to the pan.
Cover, then simmer for 20 minutes longer.
3 Grate the onions, catching the juices. Add the
chopped tomatoes, tomato paste, and the onion
and simmer gently for 30 minutes, stirring from
time to time.
4 Beat the flour into ⅔ cup (150ml) of cold water,
making sure that there are no lumps in the final
mixture. Fifteen minutes before serving, stir the
flour and water mixture into the harira. Cook
uncovered for 10 minutes, stirring continuously,
until the soup has thickened.
5 Pour in the olive oil and lemon juice and sprinkle
in the chopped parsley and cilantro. Cook gently for
another 2–3 minutes. Garnish each serving with a
lemon wedge and a teaspoon of fiery harissa.

SOUPE AUX MOULES
Mussel soup

This is a delicate yellow broth made from the cooking liquid of mussels, studded with vermicelli and small, sweet orange mussels, and flecked with basil. It looks as good as it tastes.

INGREDIENTS
4lb (2kg) mussels
bouquet garni made up of 1 fresh bay leaf and 2 sprigs each of fresh parsley, thyme, and fennel
8 cups (2 liters) shellfish stock (see page 155) or water
3 tbsp olive oil
1 onion, chopped
2 garlic cloves, finely chopped
1lb (500g) plum tomatoes, peeled, seeded, and chopped
good pinch of saffron
3oz (90g) vermicelli, broken up
salt and black pepper
good handful of basil leaves, torn
juice of ½ lemon

PREPARATION
1 Clean the mussels (see page 153). Place the bouquet garni in the stock or water and bring to a boil. Add the mussels. Cook for 4 minutes, shaking the pan occasionally, until the mussels have opened. Pour the liquid into a bowl, discarding the bouquet garni, and let the mussels cool.
2 Heat the oil in a heavy pan large enough to hold the mussel liquid. Add the onion and garlic, and fry gently for 10 minutes.
3 Add the tomatoes. Cook for 5 minutes longer over gentle heat, stirring occasionally, until the tomatoes have broken down.
4 Strain the mussel liquid through cheesecloth to remove any grit, then pour it into the pan with the tomato mixture and bring to a boil.
5 Add the saffron, vermicelli, and the seasoning (be careful with the salt as the mussel liquid will already be quite salty). Simmer, uncovered, for 10–15 minutes, until the vermicelli is cooked.
6 Meanwhile, pick the mussels out of their shells, discarding any shells that have failed to open. Take the pan off the heat and stir in the torn basil leaves and the cooked mussels.
7 Finish the soup with a squeeze of lemon and serve immediately. Do not bring the soup back to a boil or the mussels will toughen.

VARIATION
• Replace the basil leaves with 2 tablespoons of freshly made Pesto (see page 42).

AVGOLEMONO SOUPA
Chicken soup with eggs and lemon

This simple Greek soup of chicken broth with rice is made special by the last-minute addition of eggs to enrich and thicken, and lemon juice to give sharpness. The result is both refreshing and nourishing.

INGREDIENTS
6 cups (1.5 liters) chicken stock (see page 155)
¼ cup (45g) long-grain rice, rinsed and drained
salt
2 large eggs, plus 1 egg yolk
juice of 1 lemon

PREPARATION
1 Bring the stock to a boil. Add the rice to the stock, together with a pinch of salt. Boil uncovered for 10–15 minutes, until the rice is tender.
2 Beat together the whole eggs, the egg yolk, and the lemon juice. Add 4 tbsp of the hot stock to this mixture, and rapidly whisk together until thoroughly combined and smooth.
3 Take the soup off the heat and whisk in the egg and lemon mixture, being careful not to let it curdle. Beat for 2 minutes, until you have a slightly thickened, creamy soup. Serve immediately.

FIRST COURSES AND SNACKS

The people of the Mediterranean are hospitable and rarely offer a glass of wine without a little dish of delicacies to nibble on. Whether it is *tapas* in Spain, *meze* in Greece and Turkey, or *antipasti* in Italy, there is a vast selection of light appetizers to choose from. Many Mediterranean dips and spreads for bread are ideal to serve with drinks, as well as for first courses. For more substantial snacks, try Pan Bagnat or Mozzarella in Carrozza, a deep-fried cheese sandwich originally from the south of Italy.

ALLIOLI

Garlic and olive oil sauce

The Catalans make Allioli with nothing but garlic and olive oil and scorn the Provençals up the coast who use egg yolks to help bind the emulsion. Allioli can simply be spread on bread, but is especially good served as a dip with a selection of raw sliced vegetables.

INGREDIENTS

6 plump garlic cloves
1 tsp salt
¾ cup (175ml) extra-virgin olive oil

PREPARATION

1 Make sure all the ingredients are at room temperature. Crush the garlic and the salt using a mortar and pestle until you have a smooth paste.
2 Add just a drop of oil to the paste and continue to pound until it has been thoroughly incorporated.
3 Continue to add the oil drop by drop, pounding all the time, until an emulsion begins to form. If you add the oil too quickly, the mixture will not emulsify. Conversely, once you have achieved a thick emulsion, stop adding oil at once, or you will "break" the emulsification. This sauce should not be chilled before serving.

VARIATIONS

• Add 2 egg yolks (making sure they are at room temperature) to the garlic paste in the mortar. This makes the sauce much easier to prepare. However, bear in mind that raw eggs may carry a risk of salmonella infection.
• Add 1 tablespoon of fresh white bread crumbs to the garlic paste to help thicken the sauce.

TAPENADE

Olive and caper paste

Every cook in Provence has a family recipe for this intensely flavored spread. Canned tuna and anchovies are sometimes included, the herbs and spices vary, but the essentials are the small black olives of the region and the pickled buds from the caper bush.

INGREDIENTS

½ cup (125g) capers, preferably packed in salt
1 cup (250g) pitted small black olives, preferably niçoise
pinch of dried thyme
½ dried bay leaf, crumbled
1 clove, ground
salt and black pepper
½ cup (125ml) extra-virgin olive oil
squeeze of fresh lemon juice
1 baguette

PREPARATION

1 Soak the capers in water for 1 hour, with a change of water, if preserved in salt (those in vinegar require only 20 minutes soaking). Drain the capers and dry on paper towels.
2 Place the capers in a food processor with the remaining ingredients, except the baguette, and blend to a smooth paste.
3 Cut the baguette into ¾in (1.5cm) slices. Toast both sides until golden brown, spread one side with the paste, and serve. Any remaining tapenade will keep for several days in the refrigerator if covered with a thin layer of oil.

VARIATION

• Spread tapenade on halved hard-boiled eggs.

ANCHOÏADE

Anchovy paste

The people of the South of France are addicted to anchovies and for centuries have preserved the catch in vast barrels of salt to make sure they can have a continual supply of them.

INGREDIENTS

3½oz (100g) anchovy fillets, preferably packed in salt
2 garlic cloves
black pepper
4 tbsp olive oil
1 tbsp red wine vinegar
1 baguette

PREPARATION

1 Drain the salted anchovies and soak them in water for 10 minutes to remove excess saltiness (this is not necessary if using anchovies in olive oil).
2 Crush the garlic using a mortar and pestle, then add the anchovies and a good pinch of pepper and pound to a paste (this can also be done in a food processor, but with less satisfactory results).
3 Slowly add the oil, pounding continuously or keeping the food processor on until the mixture emulsifies. Finally, stir in the vinegar.
4 Slice the baguette and toast the slices, then spread them with the salty paste.

VARIATION

• To make a simple hors d'oeuvre, spread anchoïade on quarters of ripe tomatoes and hard-boiled eggs.

DUKKAH

Egyptian roasted spice and nut mix

Even if you could afford only the simplest dinner of bread and oil, a little pile of this spicy mix would make your meal enjoyable. Make it in large amounts and store in airtight containers. Serve it as a dip with bread and fruity olive oil.

INGREDIENTS

7 tbsp (100g) sesame seeds
1 tbsp (30g) cumin seeds
1½ tbsp (45g) coriander seeds
⅓ cup (60g) shelled, skinned hazelnuts
⅓ cup (60g) roasted chickpeas, optional
1 tsp salt
½ tsp black pepper

PREPARATION

1 Place a heavy frying pan over moderate heat. When the pan is hot, add the sesame seeds and stir constantly until they are lightly browned all over – take care that they do not burn.
2 Set the sesame seeds aside to cool. In the same pan, toast the cumin seeds until lightly browned and the coriander seeds until they start to pop. Toast the hazelnuts until browned all over. Let cool.
3 Mix together the seeds, nuts, and chickpeas, if using, with the salt and pepper. Pour the mixture into a food processor or coffee grinder and grind until you have a dry, powdery mix.

PAN BAGNAT

Salade niçoise in a roll

Pan bagnat *literally means "wet bread." Originally it
was simply a salade niçoise to which stale bread had
been added, weighted down, and left to absorb
the delicious juice of the tomatoes and the pungent
olive oil. But the salad was such a favorite
midmorning snack with farm workers that it was
soon served in rolls, so that it could easily be carried
into the fields and vineyards. I can't think of anything
better for a picnic on a sunny day.*

INGREDIENTS

6 large ripe plum tomatoes, quartered
salt
1 large cucumber
2 green peppers, halved, cored, and seeded
1 red onion
8oz (250g) baby fava beans, shelled
3 hard-boiled eggs
½lb (250g) tuna in olive oil
2oz (60g) anchovy fillets, preferably packed in salt
4 large round country bread rolls, such as ciabatta
1 garlic clove
1 tbsp red wine vinegar
2 tbsp olive oil
½ cup (125g) small black olives, preferably niçoise
good handful of basil leaves, torn
black pepper

PREPARATION

1 Sprinkle the tomatoes with salt and let stand
for 10 minutes.
2 Using a potato peeler, remove the skin from the
cucumber and peppers. Finely slice the cucumber
and cut the pepper into thin strips. Peel the onion,
cut in half, and slice into fine half-moons.
3 Blanch the fava beans for 1 minute in boiling
water, then slip off the tough outer skins.
4 Peel the hard-boiled eggs and cut into quarters.
5 Drain the tuna. Drain the anchovies and soak
them in water for 10 minutes to remove excess
saltiness (this is not necessary if using anchovies in
olive oil). Reserve 2 anchovies and chop the rest.
6 Rinse the tomatoes. Mix together the
cucumber, peppers, onion, and fava beans.
7 Cut the rolls in half. Scoop out the centers to
make eight bread shells. Cut the garlic clove in half
and rub the insides of the bread shells with the cut
side. Sprinkle with vinegar and olive oil.
8 Pile in the vegetable mixture, arrange the
tomatoes and eggs on top, and scatter over the
tuna and olives. Sprinkle with shredded basil leaves
and pepper. Finish with half an anchovy.

Hard-boiled
eggs

Fava beans

Red onion

Green peppers

Cucumber

Salt

Tomatoes

*Ciabatta
rolls*

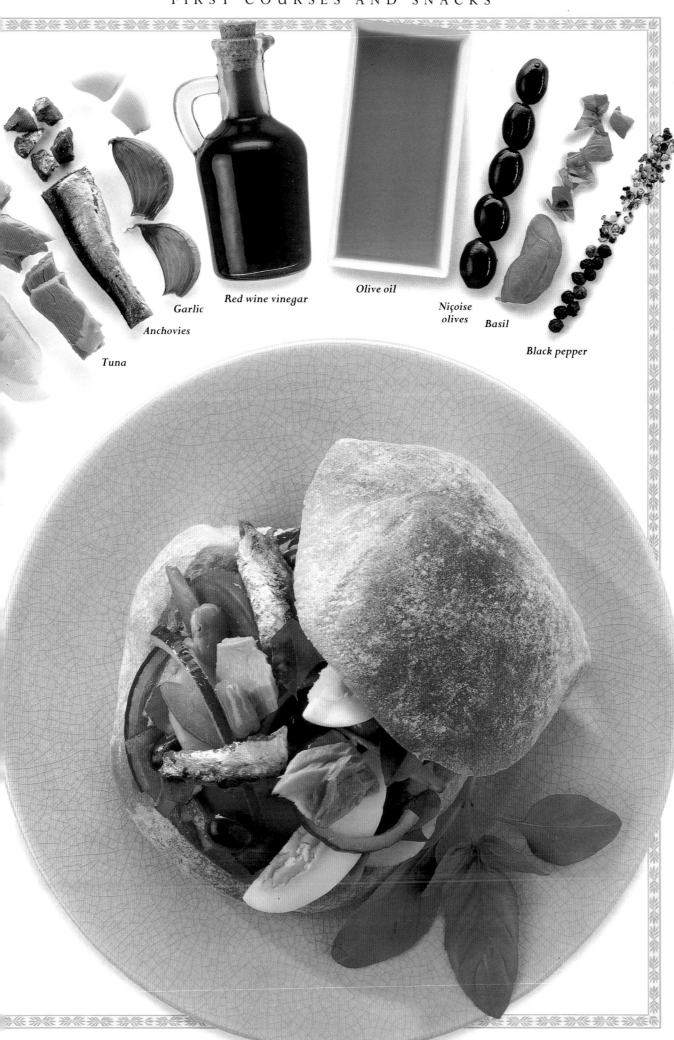

Tuna

Anchovies

Garlic

Red wine vinegar

Olive oil

Niçoise olives

Basil

Black pepper

BABA GHANOUJ

Lebanese purée of grilled eggplant

Illustrated on page 44.

INGREDIENTS

3 large eggplant
2 garlic cloves, crushed
juice of 3 lemons
⅔ cup (150ml) tahini
salt
1 tsp ground cumin
6 black olives

PREPARATION

1 Broil the eggplant under a hot grill for 20 minutes, turning them regularly until the skin is blackened and blistered all over. Cover with a clean dish towel for 10 minutes, then peel off the skin. Squeeze the eggplant flesh to remove the bitter juices.
2 Using a food processor or blender, purée the eggplant with the garlic, lemon juice, tahini, salt, and cumin. Check the balance of flavors – you may need to add more lemon juice or salt. Garnish with olives and serve.

HUMMUS BI TAHINI

Chickpea and sesame dip

Illustrated on page 44.

INGREDIENTS

1 cup (175g) dried chickpeas, soaked overnight
juice of 2 lemons
⅔ cup (150ml) tahini paste
2 garlic cloves
salt
1 tsp sweet paprika
2 tbsp olive oil
1 tbsp chopped fresh parsley

PREPARATION

1 Bring a large pan of water to a boil and add the drained chickpeas. Boil for 10 minutes, reduce the heat, and simmer for 1½ hours, until the chickpeas are very soft.
2 Using a food processor, purée the chickpeas with the lemon juice, tahini, garlic, and salt to taste. The result should be a smooth, slightly grainy paste. Taste to check the balance of lemon juice and salt.
3 Arrange the hummus in a small bowl or on a plate. Just before serving, mix the paprika into the oil and drizzle it over the hummus in a swirl. Finally, sprinkle with the chopped parsley.

TSATSIKI

Greek yogurt and cucumber dip

Illustrated on page 44.

INGREDIENTS

2 cucumbers, peeled and diced
salt
2 garlic cloves
2 cups (600ml) thick plain yogurt, preferably
sheep's or goat's milk yogurt
2 tsp dried mint

PREPARATION

1 Place the cucumber in a colander and sprinkle generously with salt. Let drain for 45 minutes, then rinse and pat dry with paper towels.
2 Using a mortar and pestle, or a teaspoon, crush the garlic with a little salt.
3 Mix the garlic into the yogurt, followed by the mint. Finally add the cucumber. Chill well.

FUL MEDAMES

Stewed beans

The traditional Egyptian breakfast, Ful Medames is something of an acquired taste first thing in the morning, given its pungent flavorings. But it makes a simple, comforting snack at other times of the day.

INGREDIENTS

¾ cup (300g) dried Egyptian brown beans or
fava beans, soaked overnight
salt
GARNISHES
olive oil
3 lemons, quartered
2 garlic cloves, crushed and chopped
2 tbsp ground cumin
4 tbsp chopped fresh parsley

PREPARATION

1 Bring twice the volume of water to beans to a boil and add the beans. Simmer for 1½–2 hours, until the beans are soft, but not falling apart – the precise time will depend on the size and age of the beans. Add salt and a little boiling water, if needed, but the finished mixture should not be too soupy.
2 Put the garnishes in small bowls so that your guests can season to taste.

VARIATION

• Serve with quartered hard-boiled eggs, sliced tomatoes, and red onions.

MOZZARELLA IN CARROZZA

Deep-fried mozzarella sandwiches

The Neapolitans claim as their own this snack of mozzarella in its bread "carriage," alluding to the famous carriages of Naples that once crisscrossed the old city.

INGREDIENTS

½lb (200g) mozzarella (drained weight)
8 thin slices slightly stale white country-style bread,
crusts removed
½ cup (125ml) whole milk
4 anchovy fillets
black pepper
4 tbsp all-purpose flour
2 eggs, beaten
oil for deep-frying, preferably olive oil

PREPARATION

1 Cut the mozzarella into 4 slices approximately ½in (1cm) thick. Trim the bread slices so they are 1in (2.5cm) larger all around than a slice of cheese.
2 Dip one side of each piece of bread into the milk. Lay a slice of mozzarella on the dry side of the bread, drape an anchovy over it, add plenty of pepper, and lay another piece of bread on top, dry side down. Press the edges of the sandwich together to seal. Repeat this process with the remaining slices of bread and mozzarella.
3 Dip each sandwich in flour and then in the beaten egg, making sure it is well coated.
4 Pour oil to a depth of 1in (2.5cm) into a pan large enough to hold all 4 sandwiches, and heat. When the oil is hot but not smoking, add the sandwiches. Fry until crisp, turning once, drain on paper towels, and serve hot.

BRIK A L'OEUF

Fried pastries with egg and tuna

This Tunisian snack takes a while to prepare, but it's worth the effort when you bite into the crisp golden pastry to find lightly cooked egg yolk.

INGREDIENTS

2 tbsp olive oil
2 onions, finely chopped
8oz (250g) tuna in olive oil
salt
pinch of cayenne
4 tbsp finely chopped fresh parsley
sunflower or vegetable oil for frying
6 sheets phyllo pastry
4 small eggs

PREPARATION

1 Heat the olive oil and fry the onion over a low heat for 10 minutes, until soft. Drain the tuna and mash it with a fork. Combine the softened onions, tuna, salt, cayenne, and parsley.
2 Pour sunflower or vegetable oil to a depth of 1in (2.5cm) into a deep frying pan and heat gently.
3 Cut 2 sheets of pastry in half. Lay out a whole sheet of pastry and place a half sheet across one end. Keep the remainder covered with a damp dish towel.
4 Place 2 tablespoons of tuna mixture on the double end of pastry and break an egg over it. Fold the unfilled pastry over the top to make an oblong shape, taking care not to press on it.
5 Slip the pastry into the hot but not smoking oil. Fry for 3–4 minutes, turning once. Drain on paper towels. Repeat with the remaining ingredients until you have four pastries. Serve immediately.

CROSTINI DI FEGATO

Tuscan chicken liver toasts

A popular antipasto, crostini are pieces of toasted bread topped with a savory spread – here a chicken liver paste.

INGREDIENTS

½lb (250g) fresh chicken livers
2 tsp butter
1 tbsp olive oil
1 small clove garlic, chopped
2 fresh sage leaves, finely chopped or pinch dried sage
salt and black pepper
squeeze of lemon
½ ciabatta loaf
1 tbsp very finely chopped fresh parsley

PREPARATION

1 Wash the chicken livers well, removing any greenish-tinged pieces, then chop them coarsely.
2 Melt the butter with the oil in a frying pan over high heat. Add the garlic, and as soon as it starts to sizzle throw in the chicken livers, sage, and seasoning. Fry for 2–3 minutes, stirring constantly, until the livers are browned.
3 Remove the pan from the heat, add the lemon juice, and mash the mixture with a fork to make a smooth paste.
4 Cut the ciabatta in half lengthwise, then cut into bite-size squares. Toast the squares until golden on both sides. Spread the surface of each square with some of the chicken liver mixture, sprinkle with parsley, and serve.

FALAFEL

Chickpea fritters

Illustrated on page 45.

INGREDIENTS

1½ cups (250g) dried chickpeas, soaked overnight
1 small red onion, chopped
2 garlic cloves, chopped
2 tsp ground coriander
2 tsp ground cumin
½ tsp cayenne
1 tsp salt
½ tsp baking powder
3 tbsp chopped fresh parsley or cilantro
sunflower or vegetable oil for deep-frying

PREPARATION

1 Drain the chickpeas and grind to a fine paste in a food processor. Add the onion and garlic and briefly process again.
2 Stir in the spices, salt, baking powder, and parsley, and process again. It is important that the paste should be very fine.
3 Pour oil to a depth of 1in (2.5cm) into a pan and heat (it is ready when a cube of bread dropped in turns golden). Form the paste into small patties and drop them into the oil. Fry for 3–4 minutes, until golden. Drain on paper towels, and serve hot.

BÖREKS

Turkish pastries

Illustrated on page 45.

INGREDIENTS

6oz (175g) feta cheese (drained weight)
2 tbsp finely chopped fresh chives or dill
2 tbsp finely chopped fresh parsley
½ tsp black pepper
6 tbsp (90g) unsalted butter
8 sheets phyllo pastry

PREPARATION

1 Crumble the feta, then mix with the herbs and pepper. Preheat the oven to 350°F (180°C).
2 Melt the butter and skim off any foam.
3 Cut the phyllo pastry into 3in (7cm) strips. Take one strip and cover the rest with a damp dish towel.
4 Brush the strip with melted butter and place a teaspoon of feta mixture on the bottom right-hand corner, as shown on page 151, and fold.
5 Lay the pastries on a baking sheet and brush with more butter. Bake for 20 minutes, until golden.

DOLMATHES

Greek stuffed grape leaves

Illustrated on page 45 and opposite.

INGREDIENTS

8oz (250g) grape leaves in brine
(approximately 40 leaves)
⅔ cup (150ml) olive oil
1 bunch scallions, including green tops
2½ cups (600ml) chicken stock (see page 155)
salt
1 cup (175g) long-grain white rice,
rinsed and drained
1 tsp ground cinnamon
2 tbsp pine nuts
½ cup (90g) raisins
juice of 1 lemon
1 fresh bay leaf
3 tbsp chopped fresh parsley
2 tbsp chopped fresh dill
1 tsp dried mint
2 lemons, cut into wedges, to serve

PREPARATION

1 Drain the grape leaves and place in a large bowl. Pour over just enough boiling water to cover them and soak for 20 minutes.
2 Heat 2 tbsp of oil in a covered saucepan. Finely chop the scallions. Add to the pan and sauté for 5 minutes, until soft. Meanwhile bring the chicken stock to a boil, adding salt to taste.
3 Add the rice and cinnamon to the saucepan and stir well, making sure the grains of rice are coated with oil. Pour in the boiling stock and simmer, covered, for 10 minutes, until all the liquid has been absorbed and small holes begin to appear in the surface of the rice.
4 Add the pine nuts and raisins to the rice, take the saucepan off the heat, cover with a dry dish towel, place the lid on top, and let stand for 15 minutes.
5 Drain the grape leaves and rinse well under cold running water. Line the base of a large heavy pan with leaves. Uncover the rice mixture and stir in half the lemon juice, the fresh herbs, and dried mint.
6 To make each *dolma*, place a grape leaf on a board, stalk end toward you, and fill and roll up, as shown opposite. Place each dolma seam side down in the pan, packing them tightly against each other.
7 Pour the remaining oil and lemon juice into the pan. Add just enough water to cover the dolmathes. Place a plate on top and weight it down. Set the pan over gentle heat and cook for 1 hour.
8 Let the dolmathes cool in the liquid before lifting them out. Serve with wedges of lemon.

STUFFING A GRAPE LEAF

1 *Place the grape leaf stalk end toward you. Put a teaspoon of rice just above the point where the stalk joins the leaf.*

2 *Using your finger and thumb, fold both sides of the grape leaf in toward the center to hold in the stuffing.*

3 *Firmly roll up the leaf from the stalk end to make a cylinder, keeping the sides tucked in and the stuffing intact.*

VEGETABLE DISHES

One of the many reasons that the Mediterranean way of eating is good for you is the heavy emphasis on vegetables. They may be served as a first course, such as the classic Provençal Ratatouille, or can follow a meat or fish course. Many make excellent main dishes, such as Parmigiana, a dish of eggplant baked with cheese, or Yemistes Piperies, Greek stuffed peppers. Although vegetables are rarely served alongside the main course in the Mediterranean, many of the following dishes make superb accompaniments to plain grilled meat or fish.

SALATA JAZAR

Carrot salad

Larger late-season carrots work best for this vibrantly colored purée pepped up with spices. As any Moroccan cook will tell you, the balance of spicing is highly individual — taste and alter the amounts to your own satisfaction.

INGREDIENTS

salt
1lb (500g) carrots
1 tsp sweet paprika
¼ tsp cayenne
½ tsp ground cumin
¼ tsp ground cinnamon
½ tsp black pepper
½ tsp sugar
juice of ½ lemon
¼ cup (60ml) olive oil
4 black olives

PREPARATION

1 Bring a large pan of heavily salted water to a boil. Peel the carrots and cook them whole for 15 minutes, or until tender, then drain.
2 Roughly chop the carrots and place them in a food processor, along with the spices, sugar, and lemon juice. Purée until smooth, then slowly add the oil, beating, or keeping the processor on, to blend it thoroughly.
3 When all the oil has been incorporated, taste the mixture to check the balance of flavors — you may need to adjust the seasoning, or add sugar or lemon juice, depending on the sweetness of the carrots. Chill for 2 hours and serve garnished with black olives.

SALATA IL SHAMONDER

Beet salad

Provided that beets are young and therefore small, they take little time to cook from their raw state — and what a difference in taste from the familiar root pickled in sharp vinegar. This Syrian dish should convince those skeptical of the merits of beets that this vegetable is really worth the effort.

INGREDIENTS

1½lb (750g) raw young beets
1 small mild onion, finely chopped
1 garlic clove, finely chopped
2 tbsp chopped fresh parsley
juice of ½ lemon
⅓ cup (90ml) olive oil
salt and black pepper

PREPARATION

1 Preheat the oven to 350°F (180°C).
2 Wash the beets and bake in their skins for 1 hour, until wrinkled and soft. Alternatively, boil them in their skins — small beets will need about 30 minutes. As soon as they are cool enough to handle, peel and dice the beets and mix with the onion, garlic, and parsley.
3 Beat together the lemon juice and oil and season well. Pour this dressing over the beets and let cool. Even though the salad is served cool, it is important to dress the beets while still warm.

VARIATIONS

• Dress the beets with a mixture of 1 cup (250ml) of yogurt and 2 tbsp of olive oil.
• Purée the salad in a food processor, rather than serving the beets diced.

SALATA HORIATIKI
Peasant salad

There are many versions of this colorful Greek salad, but it must always include crumbly sheep's milk feta, sprinkled with oregano and kalamata olives.

INGREDIENTS

2 cucumbers
salt
4 large tomatoes, peeled
½ tsp sugar
1 romaine lettuce heart
1 bunch scallions
6oz (175g) feta cheese (drained weight)
2 tsp dried oregano (rigani)
2 tbsp capers, rinsed and drained
2 tbsp chopped fresh dill
16 kalamata olives
juice of 1 lemon
½ cup (125ml) extra-virgin olive oil

PREPARATION

1 Peel the cucumbers. Cut them in half lengthwise and then across into fine half-moons. Place the cucumber slices in a colander and sprinkle with salt. Set aside for 20 minutes.

2 Cut the tomatoes in half and then slice into half-moons. Sprinkle the slices of tomato with salt and sugar and set them aside with the cucumber slices (this process helps intensify the flavor).

3 Shred the lettuce. Finely chop the scallions and lightly crumble the feta cheese. Rinse the cucumber slices and dry well on paper towels.

4 Choose a large round serving dish and make an outer circle of lettuce. Arrange the tomatoes in a ring inside, and then make an inner ring of cucumber. Pile the feta cheese in the center, then sprinkle with oregano.

5 Scatter the capers, dill, scallions, and olives over the salad. Whisk the lemon juice and oil together and pour this dressing over the salad just before serving.

ENSALADA SEVILLANA

Sevillian salad

This composed salad earns its Sevillian name through the inclusion of ingredients for which the area is famous – oranges and fat green manzanilla olives stuffed with anchovies. Illustrated on page 82.

INGREDIENTS

1 head lettuce, such as curly endive or oakleaf
2 oranges, peeled
½ red onion
1 tbsp capers, rinsed and drained
⅓ cup (90g) manzanilla olives stuffed with anchovies
1 garlic clove
yolk of 1 hard-boiled egg
2 tbsp sherry vinegar
salt and black pepper
½ cup (125ml) olive oil
1 tbsp chopped fresh tarragon

PREPARATION

1 Shred the lettuce and wash and dry it well. Cut the oranges across into thin slices. Slice the onion into fine half-moons.
2 Arrange the lettuce in a salad bowl, scatter with the orange pieces, and then sprinkle over the red onion, capers, and stuffed olives.
3 Crush the garlic using a mortar and pestle, transfer it to a small bowl, and mash it with the egg yolk until you have a smooth paste.
4 Beat in the vinegar and a good grinding of salt and pepper. Drip in the oil slowly, beating continuously to amalgamate it thoroughly. Finish the dressing with a scattering of fresh tarragon, pour it over the salad, and serve.

ANGINARES ME KOUKIA

Salad of artichokes with baby fava beans

Artichokes and fava beans are in season at the same time and Greek cooks have always combined them. Choose baby fava beans and always remove the bitter outer skins.

INGREDIENTS

½lb (250g) baby fava beans in the pod
4 small globe artichokes
1 small bunch scallions, including green tops
⅓ cup (90ml) olive oil
2 garlic cloves, finely chopped
juice of ½ lemon
salt and black pepper
3 tbsp chopped fresh parsley

PREPARATION

1 Shell the beans and slip off the tough outer skins. Prepare the artichokes (see page 150), cut the hearts in half across or in quarters, then put them in water containing lemon juice to prevent discoloration.
2 Chop the scallions into ½in (1cm) pieces. In a large, wide pan gently heat the oil with the scallions and garlic. Cook for 5 minutes, then add the artichokes, turning to coat them with oil.
3 Add the lemon juice, seasoning, and ¾ cup (175ml) of water. Bring to a slow simmer, cover the pan, and cook for 10 minutes.
4 Add the beans and most of the parsley, reserving a little for garnish. Cover and simmer for 20 minutes longer, until almost all the liquid has disappeared and the artichokes and beans are tender. Serve just warm or cool, scattered with the remaining parsley.

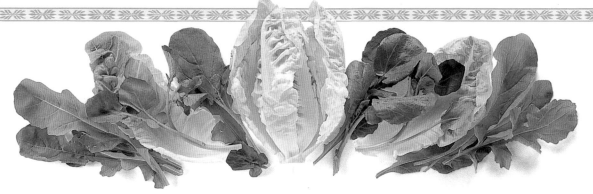

MESCLUN

Salad of young leaves

The people of the Mediterranean occasionally wander out in early summer to pick the bittersweet weeds of the fields and hillsides. The Provençal name for this selection of salad leaves comes from the Latin for "miscellany." Basically, anything goes provided it tastes good.

INGREDIENTS

1 bunch (125g) arugula
¼lb (125g) young dandelion leaves, purslane, or watercress
2 small lettuce hearts or 1 large oakleaf lettuce heart
⅓ cup (90ml) olive oil
juice of ½ lemon
salt and black pepper
4 tbsp chopped fresh chervil

PREPARATION

1 Wash all the leaves well and dry thoroughly, discarding any discolored or wilted leaves.
2 Whisk together the olive oil and lemon juice with plenty of seasoning. Mix in the chervil. Dress the salad just before serving.

MANITARIA AFELIA

Mushrooms in red wine with coriander seeds

The Cypriots have a particular addiction to coriander seeds, the orange scent of which perfumes this dish of mushrooms cooked in red wine. It can be served as an appetizer, part of a meze selection, or with grilled meat.

INGREDIENTS

½lb (250g) small mushrooms
¼ cup (60ml) olive oil
½ cup (125ml) red wine
salt and black pepper
1 tbsp coriander seeds, crushed

PREPARATION

1 Wipe the mushrooms clean, avoiding washing them if possible. Heat the olive oil over medium heat and add the mushrooms. Cook, stirring continuously, for 5 minutes, until browned all over.
2 Pour the wine into the pan, allow to boil hard for 1 minute, then turn down to a simmer. Season and cook uncovered for 8 minutes. Add the coriander seeds and cook for 2 minutes longer. Let cool slightly before serving.

CARCIOFI ALLA GIUDEA

Artichokes Jewish style

In many Mediterranean cities an individual style of cooking has developed in the Jewish community. Rome is no exception, and this dish of baby purple artichokes stewed in olive oil is now a favorite traditional dish throughout the town. Illustrated on page 83.

INGREDIENTS

12 very small and tender globe artichokes, stalks attached
2 lemons
8 garlic cloves, peeled
salt and black pepper
olive oil for stewing
2 tbsp finely chopped fresh parsley
1 tbsp finely chopped fresh mint

PREPARATION

1 Pull off the tough outer leaves of the artichokes and trim the stalks, leaving 2in (5cm) intact. Cut in half lengthwise and scoop out any choke. (Note that very small artichokes will have barely any choke.) Place the half-artichokes in water mixed with lemon juice to prevent discoloration.
2 Place the garlic cloves in a heavy pan into which the drained artichokes fit snugly. Add plenty of salt and pepper and then pour in just enough olive oil to cover the artichokes. Cover the saucepan and place over very low heat. Cook gently for 45 minutes – the artichokes should stew slowly, not fry, in the oil.
3 Drain the artichokes, reserving the flavored oil for later use. Let cool, then sprinkle with the chopped herbs. Serve with lemon wedges.

CAPONATA

Sweet and sour eggplant, onion, and celery salad

*Tradition has that this dish was introduced to Sicily
by the Moors, who needed to preserve their vegetables for
sea voyages. They may have been forbidden to drink wine,
but they made plentiful use of wine vinegar. The
surviving dish is a delicate balance of Mediterranean
vegetables in a sweet and sour sauce. It is sometimes
served sprinkled with grated bitter chocolate.*

INGREDIENTS

1¼lb (625g) eggplant
salt
1 onion
1¼ cups (300ml) olive oil
3 ribs celery, including leaves
1lb (500g) ripe plum tomatoes, peeled and chopped
½ cup (125ml) red wine vinegar
1 tbsp sugar
½ cup (125g) cracked green olives
1 tbsp capers, rinsed and drained
black pepper
2 tbsp chopped fresh parsley

PREPARATION

1 Cut the eggplant into 1in (2.5cm) round
slices, then cut each slice into quarters. Salt
and blot them (see page 150).
2 Peel the onion, cut in half, and slice into fine
half-moons. Heat 2 tbsp of oil in a wide skillet and
cook the onion gently for 10 minutes, until
translucent and soft.
3 Dice the celery and add to the onion along with
the chopped celery leaves. Cook for 10 minutes
longer, stirring frequently. Add the tomatoes and
cook for 5 minutes longer.
4 Pour in the vinegar and stir in the sugar. Add the
olives and capers. Simmer for 10 minutes, until the
tomatoes have broken down to form a thick sauce.
5 Pour the remaining oil into a skillet to a depth
of 1in (2.5cm) and warm over medium heat. When
the oil is very hot, add the rinsed and dried eggplant
pieces. Cook for 5 minutes, stirring from time to
time, until they are browned on all sides. Remove
with a slotted spoon and drain on paper towels.
6 Stir the eggplant pieces into the tomato and
celery mixture. Taste to check the balance of sweet
and sour flavors – you may need to add a little
more sugar. Season generously and then stir in the
chopped parsley.
7 Let the salad stand for 24 hours (preferably not
in the refrigerator) to allow the flavors to mingle
before serving.

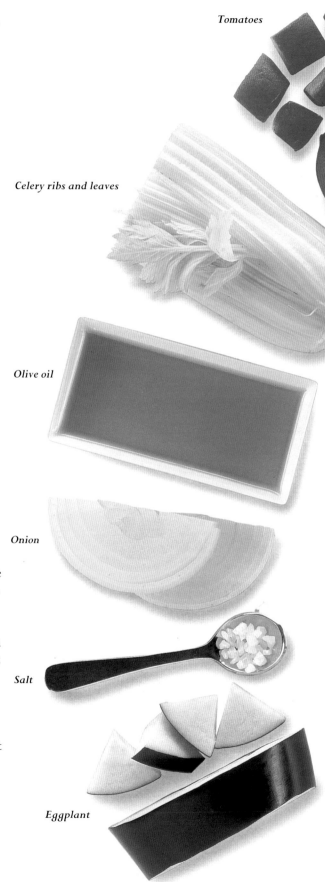

Tomatoes

Celery ribs and leaves

Olive oil

Onion

Salt

Eggplant

Red wine
vinegar

Sugar

Cracked
green olives

Capers

Black
pepper

Parsley

PEPERONATA

Stewed peppers

Glossy with olive oil, red with tomato, this simple Italian dish brings out the best in sweet peppers. Prepare it several hours in advance to allow the flavors to develop.

INGREDIENTS

4 large mixed red and green peppers, cored and seeded
½ cup (100ml) olive oil
1 onion, finely chopped
2 garlic cloves, finely chopped
1¼lb (625g) plum tomatoes, peeled, seeded, and chopped
14oz (425g) can whole peeled tomatoes, chopped
salt and black pepper

PREPARATION

1 Cut the peppers into thin strips. Warm the oil in a heavy pan over low heat and add the pepper, onion, and garlic. Cover and stew for 30 minutes.
2 Add the fresh and canned tomatoes and seasoning. Leave barely simmering, uncovered, for 20 minutes. Allow to cool before serving.

ESPINACAS A LA CATALANA

Spinach Catalan style

Illustrated on page 38.

INGREDIENTS

3 tbsp raisins
4lb (2kg) fresh spinach
½ cup (100ml) olive oil, plus oil for frying
1 garlic clove, finely chopped
3 tbsp pine nuts
salt and black pepper
2 slices white bread, crusts removed, cut into triangles

PREPARATION

1 Soak the raisins in hot water while preparing the spinach. Wash the spinach well and remove any tough stalks. Bring a large pan of salted water to a boil and cook the spinach for 3 minutes. Drain the spinach, plunge it into a large bowl of cold water, and then drain again immediately.
2 Chop the spinach roughly. Put the oil in a heatproof pot and warm it over very low heat. Add the garlic, pine nuts, drained raisins, and spinach. Season well and cook for 20 minutes, stirring occasionally. Let stand for 15 minutes.
3 Meanwhile, warm some oil in a skillet over medium heat and fry the bread until golden on both sides. Serve the spinach garnished with the bread triangles.

HABAS CON JAMON

Fava beans with ham

Illustrated on page 39.

INGREDIENTS

3lb (1.5kg) baby fava beans in the pod
½ cup (100ml) olive oil
¼lb (125g) chunk Serrano ham or other cured ham, diced
salt and black pepper
2 tsp chopped fresh mint
juice of ½ lemon

PREPARATION

1 Shell the fava beans and slip off the tough outer skins, revealing the bright green halves of the bean.
2 Warm the oil in a heavy pan, preferably earthenware, over medium heat. Add the beans and cook for 10 minutes.
3 Add the ham and seasoning (be careful with the salt as cured ham is already salty), then stir in the mint. Cook for 2–3 minutes longer before sprinkling with lemon juice.

CIPOLLINE IN AGRODOLCE

Sweet and sour baby onions

The ancient Romans were especially fond of dishes that combined honey and vinegar for a sweet and sour flavor. The tradition continues in this dish of caramelized onions. Serve hot with roast meat or cold with salami as antipasti.

INGREDIENTS

1lb (500g) baby onions no more than 1½in (3.5cm)
in diameter
2 tbsp olive oil
2 cloves
1 bay leaf
¼ cup (60ml) red wine vinegar
1 tbsp sugar
salt and black pepper

PREPARATION

1 Bring a large pan of water to a boil. Add the onions in their skins, bring back to a boil, and cook for 5 minutes. Remove from the heat, allow to cool, then skin them, taking care to leave them whole.
2 Warm the oil in a heavy pan over medium to low heat. Add the cloves, bay leaf, and onions. Cook for 20 minutes, turning the onions until browned.
3 Increase the heat and add the vinegar and sugar. Cook for 2 minutes, until the pan juices acquire a syrupy consistency. Stir well to coat the onions, then season. Remove the cloves and bay leaf and serve.

RATATOUILLE

Vegetables stewed in olive oil

*Ratatouille may be the definitive dish of Provence,
but too often it becomes simply a vegetable stew.
The key to Ratatouille is that the vegetables, except for
the tomatoes, should hold their individual textures and
flavors. They should therefore be cooked separately before
being put together in the pot.*

INGREDIENTS

1lb (500g) eggplant
1lb (500g) zucchini
salt
1lb (500g) mild onions
1lb (500g) red peppers, cored and seeded
¾ cup (175ml) olive oil
6 garlic cloves, chopped
2lb (1kg) plum tomatoes, peeled, seeded, and chopped
3 sprigs fresh thyme
1 tbsp chopped fresh parsley
2 tbsp chopped fresh basil
4 coriander seeds
black pepper

PREPARATION

1 Cut the eggplant and zucchini across into
slices ½in (1cm) thick. Place them in separate
colanders and salt and blot (see page 150).
2 Peel the onions, cut in half, and slice into fine
half-moons. Cut the peppers into thin strips.
3 Heat half the oil in a large pan. When the oil is
hot but not smoking, add the rinsed and dried
eggplant slices and cook for 3–4 minutes on each
side, until soft and lightly browned. Remove and
drain well on paper towels. Discard the oil.
4 Heat another 4 tbsp of oil and cook the zucchini
slices over a high heat for 3–4 minutes on each
side, until lightly browned. Remove the zucchini
and place them in a heavy pan with the cooked
eggplant slices.
5 Cook the onions in the remaining oil over a low
heat for 6–8 minutes, until just soft but not
browned. Finally, cook the peppers for 5 minutes,
until the skin is lightly wrinkled. Put all the
vegetables together in the pan.
6 Heat the oil left in the pan and add the garlic.
When the garlic starts to sizzle, add the chopped
tomatoes, the herbs, coriander seeds, salt, and
pepper. Cook for 5 minutes, until the tomatoes are
on the verge of breaking down.
7 Pour the tomato mixture over the vegetables in
the pan and cook gently for 10 minutes.
8 Let cool, preferably not in the refrigerator.
Ratatouille is best served the following day.

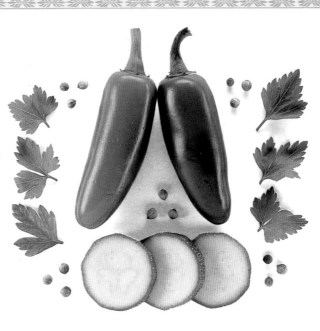

CHAKCHOUKA

Tunisian spicy peppers and tomatoes with eggs

*This dish is similar to the Basque pipperada –
with the typical Tunisian addition of hot chilies. The
eggs are left to cook whole among the vegetables. This
dish should be served straight from the pan with plenty of
bread to mop up the juices.*

INGREDIENTS

1 large onion
3 green peppers, cored and seeded
3 tbsp olive oil
1 garlic clove, finely chopped
2 small fresh green chilies, seeded and finely chopped
1¼lb (625g) plum tomatoes, peeled
salt and black pepper
4 large eggs

PREPARATION

1 Peel the onion, cut in half, and slice into fine
half-moons. Thinly slice the peppers. Warm the oil
in a large, shallow heavy-based pan with a lid over
low heat. Add the onion. Stew very gently for
15 minutes, stirring occasionally, until the onions
are soft. Do not allow them to brown.
2 Add the peppers, garlic, and chilies to the onion.
Cook for 20 minutes, until the peppers have
softened and lost their bright green appearance.
3 Cut the tomatoes in half, or in quarters if they
are large. Add them to the pan, cut side down,
and cook for 10 minutes longer, until the juices
begin to run.
4 Season well, then make 4 wells in the mixture
and carefully break a whole egg into each. Cover
the pan and cook until the eggs are just set,
6–7 minutes. Serve straight from the pan.

ENSALADA SEVILLANA
Sevillian salad
(page 76)

ESCALIVADA
Roasted peppers, eggplant, and onions
(page 88)

CARCIOFI ALLA GIUDEA
Artichokes Jewish style
(page 77)

BEIGNETS DE FLEURS DE COURGETTE

Provençal zucchini flower fritters with fresh tomato sauce. Serves 6.

INGREDIENTS

24 small zucchini flowers
¼ cup (150g) all-purpose flour
1 tsp salt
2 large eggs, separated
1 tbsp olive oil
1½ cups (350ml) whole milk
sunflower or vegetable oil for deep-frying
TOMATO SAUCE
1½lb (750g) plum tomatoes, peeled and seeded
2 tbsp olive oil
salt and black pepper
2 shallots, finely chopped
2 garlic cloves, finely chopped
1 tbsp torn fresh basil

PREPARATION

1 Carefully remove the stems and the long pistils inside the flowers.
2 Sift the flour into a large bowl. Make a well in the center and add the salt. Lightly beat the egg yolks and add them to the flour with the oil. Mix together with a wooden spoon, then beat in a little milk. Pour in the remaining milk in a steady stream while you continue to beat, until you have a smooth batter.
3 To make the sauce, put half the tomatoes in a sieve over a bowl. Press with the back of a wooden spoon to release the juice. Discard the flesh.
4 Beat the olive oil and seasoning into the tomato juice. Finely dice the remaining tomatoes and add to the juice with the shallots, garlic, and basil. Place in the refrigerator until needed.
5 Take a large saucepan or deep fryer, pour in oil to a depth of 4in (10cm), and heat. When the oil is almost ready (it is ready when a cube of bread dropped in it turns golden), whisk the egg whites until stiff and fold them into the batter.
6 Dip each flower in the batter and transfer to the hot oil. When the underside of the flower is golden (around 1 minute), turn it and fry for another minute. Never cook more than 3 flowers at a time.
7 Drain the fritters on paper towels. Serve immediately with the chilled tomato sauce.

VARIATION

• In Italy the flowers are fried in a light batter of ⅔ cup (90g) all-purpose flour to 1¼ cups (300ml) of ice water and served separately or with grilled meat.

PATATAS BRAVAS

Spicy potatoes

Only the courageous should eat these potatoes, as their name suggests. There are many different versions of this dish in Spain, but they have one common characteristic – the potatoes are always spicy hot.

INGREDIENTS

1½lb (750g) small potatoes
¼ cup (60ml) olive oil
salt and black pepper
2 tsp sweet paprika
½ tsp cayenne
2 tbsp red wine vinegar
2 tsp tomato paste

PREPARATION

1 Peel the potatoes and cut them into bite-sized chunks. Heat the oil in a heavy nonstick skillet and add the potatoes. Cook for 3–4 minutes, turning frequently, until they are lightly browned.
2 Season the potatoes, turn the heat to low, and cover the pan. Let the potatoes cook for 20 minutes, shaking the pan halfway through.
3 Turn up the heat and sprinkle the potatoes with the paprika and cayenne. Stir well to coat.
4 Mix together the vinegar and tomato paste and pour into the pan – stand back; it will spatter. Cook for 2 minutes, stirring constantly, until the potato pieces are well coated with a thick spicy sauce – there should be no liquid or oil left in the pan.

TORTILLA

Spanish potato omelet

Illustrated on page 39.

INGREDIENTS

4 large boiling potatoes
1 large Spanish onion
½ cup (125ml) olive oil
5 large eggs
salt and black pepper

PREPARATION

1 Peel the potatoes and slice them very finely across (a mandoline or food processor is useful). Peel the onion, cut in half, and slice into fine half-moons.
2 Warm three quarters of the oil in a heavy skillet over low heat. Add the potatoes and onions, cover, and cook for 30 minutes, until they are soft but not colored.
3 Remove the potatoes and onions from the pan with a slotted spoon and let cool for 10 minutes. Drain off any excess oil. Beat the eggs and season well. Add the potatoes and onions to the eggs.
4 Return the pan to a low heat and pour in 1 tbsp of oil. Add the egg, potato, and onion mix. Cook until set in the center, about 10 minutes.
5 Place an inverted plate over the pan and turn it upside down. Warm the remaining oil, slide the tortilla back in, uncooked side down, and cook for 5 minutes. Serve warm or cold, cut into wedges.

CHAMPIÑONES AL AJILLO

Spanish mushrooms with garlic

Illustrated on page 38.

INGREDIENTS

1lb (500g) mushrooms
¼ cup (60ml) olive oil
3 garlic cloves, finely chopped
salt and black pepper
juice of ½ lemon
2 tbsp chopped fresh parsley

PREPARATION

1 Clean the mushrooms – wipe wild ones with a damp cloth, rather than immersing them in water. Halve large mushrooms, but leave others whole.
2 Warm the oil in a skillet over medium heat. Add the garlic and cook for 1 minute, then add the mushrooms. Cook for 5 minutes, stirring constantly, then season. Cook for 2 minutes longer, then stir in the lemon juice and parsley.

FRITTATA DI ZUCCHINE

Zucchini omelet

Some describe the frittata as the Italian version of the omelet, but apart from its use of eggs, the principles are quite different and the result is thick and juicy. My own summer favorite is made with zucchini, but sliced artichoke hearts also taste very good.

INGREDIENTS

1 large onion
2 tbsp olive oil
1lb (500g) small zucchini
salt and black pepper
6 large eggs
½ cup (60g) freshly grated Parmesan
2 tbsp (30g) butter

PREPARATION

1 Peel the onion, cut in half, and slice into fine half-moons. Heat the oil and cook the onion gently for 20 minutes, until very soft but not browned.
2 Slice the zucchini across into ¼in (5mm) slices. Add the zucchini to the softened onion, season well, and raise the heat to medium. Cook, stirring frequently, for 5 minutes.
3 Drain off any excess oil and discard. Let the vegetables cool for 10 minutes. Meanwhile, beat the eggs with the Parmesan.
4 Stir the slightly cooled vegetable mixture into the eggs and cheese. Melt the butter in a nonstick frying pan approximately 12in (30cm) across over low heat. When the butter begins to bubble, pour in the egg and vegetable mixture. Let cook over low heat for 15 minutes.
5 Heat the broiler to medium. When the frittata is almost set, place the pan under the broiler for 2 minutes. Serve cold or hot.

YEMISTES PIPERIES

Stuffed peppers with tomato sauce

*This Greek dish represents the principles of
Mediterranean food, the main component being
vegetables, made substantial with a rice and lamb filling.
Variations using eggplant and tomatoes are also popular.*

INGREDIENTS

8 small green peppers, tops sliced off, cored, and seeded
⅓ cup (75ml) olive oil
2 onions, finely chopped
3 garlic cloves, finely chopped
3 tbsp red wine
1 tbsp honey
1 tbsp tomato paste
3lb (1.5kg) plum tomatoes, peeled and chopped
1 cinnamon stick
2 cloves
1 fresh bay leaf
salt and black pepper
1½ cups (350ml) chicken stock (see page 155)
½lb (250g) ground lamb
2 tsp ground cinnamon
2 tsp ground cumin
½ cup (125g) long-grain rice, rinsed and drained

PREPARATION

1 Bring a pan of water to a boil and cook the
peppers and tops for 5 minutes. Drain and set aside.
2 To make the sauce, heat half the oil and add half
the onion and garlic. Stew gently for 10 minutes,
until the onion is soft. Add the wine, honey, and
tomato paste. Let simmer for 1 minute.
3 Add the tomatoes, cinnamon stick, cloves, bay
leaf, and seasoning. Simmer, uncovered, for
30 minutes, until the sauce is thick.
4 Strain the sauce through a sieve and set aside.
Heat the stock to the boiling point.
5 To make the filling, warm the rest of the oil and
add the remaining onion and garlic. Cook gently
for 10 minutes, until the onion is soft. Turn up the
heat and add the lamb, ground spices, and seasoning.
Cook for 2 minutes, stirring, to brown the meat.
6 Add the rice to the lamb mixture. Stir well,
then pour over the boiling stock. Cook over gentle
heat for 15 minutes, until all the liquid has been
absorbed and small holes appear in the surface.
7 Preheat the oven to 350°F (180°C). Stuff the
peppers with the rice mixture and replace their
tops. Pack them into a dish and pour over the sauce.
Cover and bake for 1 hour. Allow to cool before
serving – this dish is best made a day in advance.

PARMIGIANA

Eggplant baked with mozzarella and Parmesan

*From Campania, the sun-baked southern tip of Italy,
comes this basil-scented dish of eggplant smothered
in tomato sauce and sandwiched between mozzarella
and Parmesan. Classically, the eggplant are fried before
being baked, but I prefer to broil them to
reduce the amount of oil in the dish.*

INGREDIENTS

*1½lb (750g) small eggplant
salt
⅓ cup (75ml) olive oil
1 onion, chopped
2 garlic cloves, finely sliced
2lb (1kg) plum tomatoes, peeled and seeded or
1¼lb (625g) canned whole peeled tomatoes
1 tsp tomato paste (omit if using canned tomatoes)
1 tsp chopped fresh oregano
black pepper
7oz (200g) mozzarella (drained weight)
1 cup (125g) freshly grated Parmesan
handful of basil leaves*

PREPARATION

1 Cut the eggplant lengthwise into ½in (1cm)
wide strips and salt and blot them (see page 150).
2 Meanwhile, make the tomato sauce. Heat 3 tbsp
of oil in a heavy pan over low heat. Add the onion
and garlic. Cook gently for 20 minutes.
3 Turn up the heat and add the tomatoes and
tomato paste, if using. Add the oregano and
seasoning and allow to bubble for 5 minutes,
stirring frequently to break down the tomatoes.
4 Preheat the broiler. Place the rinsed and dried
eggplant on a metal baking sheet, dribble over a
little oil, and broil for 5 minutes. Turn the
eggplant, dribble with the remaining oil, and broil
for 5 minutes longer. Slice the mozzarella.
5 Preheat the oven to 350°F (180°C). Take a deep
round earthenware dish and cover the base with a
layer of tomato sauce. Lay some eggplant strips on
top, followed by three quarters of the mozzarella
and half the Parmesan. Season well.
6 Add the basil leaves. Top with the remaining
eggplant and mozzarella, pour over the rest of the
tomato sauce, and sprinkle over the remainder of
the Parmesan. Bake in the oven for 30 minutes.

ESCALIVADA

Roasted peppers, eggplant, and onions

The three vegetables that comprise Escalivada are traditionally roasted over charcoal, but today most Catalans cook them in the oven. Whatever method is used, the sweetness of the vegetables is brought to the fore. For a more substantial dish, finish with a scattering of flakes of cooked tuna or salt cod. Illustrated on page 83.

INGREDIENTS

1½ lb (750g) red peppers
1½ lb (750g) eggplant
1 lb (500g) onions in their skins
salt
¼ cup (60ml) extra-virgin olive oil
1 garlic clove, finely chopped

PREPARATION

1 Preheat the oven to 350°F (180°C). Place the peppers, eggplant, and onions on a baking sheet and bake for 1 hour, or until tender.
2 Remove the sheet from the oven and cover the vegetables with a dish towel. Leave for 10 minutes.
3 Remove the blistered skin of the peppers (see page 150) and scrape out the seeds. Cut the flesh into strips. Remove the skin of the eggplant and cut the flesh lengthwise into strips. Peel the onions and roughly chop the flesh.
4 Arrange the roasted vegetables in a serving dish. Sprinkle liberally with salt and olive oil, scatter over the raw garlic, and let cool before serving.

HUEVOS REVUELTOS CON ESPARRAGOS

Scrambled egg with asparagus

I cannot imagine a more indulgent supper than this simple Spanish dish. It is traditionally made with wild green asparagus; look for the very thin stalks.

INGREDIENTS

1 lb (500g) asparagus
5 large eggs
pinch each of sweet paprika and ground cumin
salt and black pepper
2 tbsp olive oil
2 tbsp butter

PREPARATION

1 Trim the woody ends from the asparagus, removing the tough fibrous outer layer with a potato peeler if the stalks are large. Cut the asparagus into 1in (2.5cm) lengths, setting aside the tips.
2 Bring a pan of salted water to a boil and add the asparagus, excluding the tips. Boil thin stalks for 2 minutes, thicker asparagus for 4 minutes. Add the tips and boil for 2 minutes longer. Drain carefully – the asparagus should be just tender.
3 Beat the eggs with the spices and seasoning.
4 Warm the olive oil with the butter in a large heavy pan over moderate heat. When the butter has melted and the oil is sizzling, add the eggs. Stir for 1 minute with a wooden spoon, then add the asparagus. Cook for a minute longer, until the eggs are just set, and serve at once.

YOĞURTLU PATLICAN

Fried eggplant with yogurt

Thick creamy yogurt is often used in Turkey to dress raw and cooked vegetables, here fried eggplant. For a lighter dish, brush the eggplant with oil and broil them until golden brown before topping with the spicy yogurt.

INGREDIENTS

¾ lb (900g) large eggplant
salt
⅔ cup (150ml) olive oil
1¼ cups (300ml) plain yogurt, strained through cheesecloth
2 garlic cloves, peeled and crushed
1 tsp caraway seeds
salt and black pepper
½ tsp sweet paprika
1 tbsp chopped fresh dill

PREPARATION

1 Cut the eggplant across into ½ in (1cm) slices. Salt and blot them (see page 150).
2 Heat the oil in a skillet over medium-high heat. When the oil is ready (when a cube of bread dropped in it turns golden), add a few rinsed and dried eggplant slices. Cook for 1 minute on each side until golden, remove with a slotted spoon, and drain on paper towels.
3 Continue this process until all the eggplant slices are cooked. Do not add too many slices to the skillet at once and make sure that the oil is very hot or the eggplant will absorb too much oil.
4 Mix together the yogurt, garlic, caraway seeds, and seasoning. Lay the fried eggplant slices on a plate and pour over the spiced yogurt. Sprinkle with the paprika and dill. The eggplant can be served warm or cold, but should be dressed with the yogurt while still hot.

TUMBET

Baked vegetables

Rich in olive oil, this Majorcan dish makes a substantial main course and is often served on the island with slices of sausage and cured pork. In some versions, the potatoes are replaced by dried bread crumbs.

INGREDIENTS

1lb (500g) eggplant
salt
1 cup (250ml) olive oil
1lb (500g) new potatoes, peeled and sliced
1lb (500g) green peppers, cored, seeded, and cut into strips
5 garlic cloves
2½lb (1.25kg) plum tomatoes, peeled and chopped
black pepper
pinch of sugar, optional

PREPARATION

1 Slice the eggplant thinly across. Salt and blot them (see page 150).
2 Heat the oil in a large heavy skillet. When the oil is just beginning to sizzle, add the potato slices. Cook for 5 minutes, turning them frequently, until lightly browned. Remove with a slotted spoon and drain on paper towels.
3 Add the peppers to the oil and cook for 2–3 minutes, until just colored. Remove with a slotted spoon and drain on paper towels.
4 Cook the rinsed and drained eggplant in two batches in the oil, until golden on both sides. Remove and drain on paper towels.
5 Preheat the oven to 375°F (190°C). Drain off all but 2 tablespoons of the oil and return the pan to the heat. Add the garlic and, as soon as it starts to sizzle, add the tomatoes. Keep the heat high and cook the tomatoes for 5 minutes, stirring constantly, until they break down.
6 Push the resulting tomato sauce through a fine sieve and season to taste, adding a pinch of sugar if the tomatoes are not very flavorful.
7 Arrange the cooked vegetables in layers in an earthenware lidded casserole, starting with potatoes and ending with eggplant, and seasoning as you go.
8 Pour over the tomato sauce, cover the dish, and place in the preheated oven for 30 minutes. Let stand for 20 minutes before serving.

SPANAKOPITA

Spinach pie

This spiced spinach pie with an orange-flavored crust is a favorite Greek picnic dish. If you don't have time to make your own pastry, use layers of phyllo brushed with olive oil.

INGREDIENTS

PASTRY
2½ cups (300g) all-purpose flour
1 tsp salt
2 tbsp olive oil
4–5 tbsp (60–75ml) freshly squeezed orange juice
1 small egg, separated
SPINACH FILLING
1½lb (750g) spinach, washed and trimmed
¼ cup (60ml) olive oil
1 onion, finely chopped
salt and black pepper
1 tsp ground cumin
juice of 1 lemon
3 tbsp chopped fresh dill
2 tbsp sesame seeds

PREPARATION

1 To make the pastry, sift the flour and salt into a bowl. Make a well in the center and add the olive oil and orange juice. Lightly whisk the egg white, add to the flour, and work the mixture together.
2 With floured hands, knead the pastry for 5 minutes, until it loses its stickiness and becomes pliable. Wrap it in plastic wrap and chill for 1 hour.
3 Put the spinach in a pan with 2 tbsp of water, cover, and cook gently until wilted. Drain and, when cool enough to handle, squeeze dry.
4 Heat 2 tbsp of oil over low heat and add the onion. Cook for 10 minutes, until soft. Add the spinach, seasoning, cumin, lemon juice, and dill. Cook gently for 5 minutes longer, until any liquid has evaporated.
5 Preheat the oven to 350°F (180°C). Oil a 9in (23cm) tart pan. Take two thirds of the pastry and put the remainder back in the refrigerator. Dip your hands in a bowl of ice water. Flour a surface and roll out the pastry to fit the tart pan. Trim the edges and then fill the pie with the spinach mixture.
6 Roll out the remaining pastry to form a crust, sealing the edges with ice water. Brush the crust with the remainder of the oil and place in the oven.
7 After 30 minutes, turn the heat down to 300°F (150°C). Brush with beaten egg yolk and sprinkle over the sesame seeds. Return to the oven and bake for another 30 minutes, until the sesame seeds are toasted. Serve warm or cold.

FISH DISHES

The Mediterranean region is defined by its sea, and it is the fruits of that water that most characterize Mediterranean cooking. A visit to the local fish market will reveal a bewildering array of colors and shapes: tiny glinting silver fish for the frying pan, the vermilion shine of red mullet, thick steaks of tuna and swordfish, piles of tiny squid no bigger than a thumbnail. Then there are the shellfish stalls, stacked high with mussels and clams, shrimp, crabs, and lobsters of all varieties and sizes. The choice is endless and all find their way into the cooking pot.

ALMEJAS A LA MARINERA

Clams with white wine and garlic sauce

No tapas bar is complete without shellfish. There may be a few stuffed mussels, a shellfish salad, or this dish of clams cooked in a white wine and garlic sauce. The little clam shells serve as spoons for scooping up the sauce.

INGREDIENTS

2lb (1kg) small clams
⅓ cup (90ml) olive oil
1 small white onion, finely chopped
4 garlic cloves, finely chopped
1 small dried red chili, finely chopped
1 tbsp all-purpose flour
1 cup (250ml) medium-dry white wine
2 tsp sweet paprika
salt and black pepper
1 bay leaf
2 tbsp finely chopped fresh parsley

PREPARATION

1 Clean the clams (see page 153).
2 Heat the oil in an earthenware dish or a heavy pan over gentle heat. Add the onion, garlic, and chili and sauté for 15 minutes, stirring regularly, until the onion is tinged with yellow.
3 Turn up the heat to medium and add the clams. Cook until all the clams open (3–4 minutes), discarding any that have not opened, then stir in the flour, followed by the wine.
4 Add the paprika, salt and pepper to taste (be careful with the salt as the liquid the clams release is salty), the bay leaf, and parsley. Simmer for 5 minutes, stirring continuously, until the sauce has thickened. Check the seasoning and serve.

ESQUEIXADA

Salt cod salad

Salt cod, traditionally served on Fridays and during Lent, remains very popular in the west of the Mediterranean region. It needs long soaking and is often poached. In this Catalan salad, however, the salt cod is not cooked but simply marinated and shredded.

INGREDIENTS

1lb (500g) salt cod
1 green pepper, peeled, cored, and seeded
1 red pepper, peeled, cored, and seeded
1 small mild onion
1 small garlic clove
2 large tomatoes, peeled, seeded, and chopped
½ cup (125ml) olive oil
2 tbsp red wine vinegar
black pepper
½ cup (60g) small black olives

PREPARATION

1 Soak the salt cod for 24 hours, changing the water several times. Remove the skin and bone and finely shred the flesh with your fingers. Do not be tempted to use a knife.
2 Finely dice the peppers. Peel the onion and cut into very thin rings.
3 Cut the garlic clove in half and rub the cut side around an earthenware serving dish. Mix together the peppers, onion, tomatoes, and the shredded salt cod and place in the dish.
4 Beat together the oil and vinegar to form an emulsion. Add a generous grinding of pepper and pour this dressing over the salad. Marinate for at least 4 hours to allow the flavors to develop. Garnish the salad with olives before serving.

SALPICON DE MARISCOS

Spanish shellfish salad

INGREDIENTS

1½lb (750g) mussels and clams
¾lb (375g) cooked large shrimp
⅓ cup (90ml) olive oil
2 tbsp sherry vinegar
2 tbsp capers, rinsed and drained
4 cornichons, finely chopped
1 tbsp chopped bottled red pimiento pepper
½ mild white onion, chopped
2 tbsp chopped fresh parsley
salt and black pepper

PREPARATION

1 Clean the mussels and clams (see page 153). Steam them open in 4 tablespoons of water. As soon as they are cool enough to handle, remove most of them from their shells, reserving a few in their shells for a garnish, if desired. Discard any that have not opened. Peel the cooked shrimp.

2 Beat together the oil and vinegar until emulsified. Mix with the remaining ingredients. Pour this mixture over the shrimp and shelled mussels and clams, being careful to coat all the shellfish thoroughly.

3 Chill for at least 4 hours, preferably overnight, to allow the flavors to mingle before serving.

SARDALYA SARMASI
Stuffed sardines in grape leaves
(page 102)

**COQUILLES ST. JACQUES
A LA PROVENÇALE**
*Scallops with garlic
and Cognac*
(page 97)

BOUILLABAISSE
Marseillais fish stew
(page 97)

PESCE ALLA GRIGLIA SALSA VERDE

Italian grilled fish with green sauce

Illustrated on page 51.

INGREDIENTS

2lb (1kg) small red mullet or small snapper
1 cup (60g) finely chopped fresh parsley
10–12 (50g) anchovies in olive oil, drained and
finely chopped
2 tbsp capers, rinsed, drained, and finely chopped
2 garlic cloves, finely chopped
juice of 1 lemon
¾ cup (175ml) olive oil, plus oil to grease
black pepper

PREPARATION

1 Clean, scale, and gut the mullet (see page 152).
Lay them on an oiled baking sheet or barbecue rack
and preheat the broiler to maximum or make sure
the charcoals are glowing.
2 Make the salsa verde. Mix the parsley, anchovy,
capers, garlic, lemon juice, oil, and pepper.
3 Broil or grill the fish for 5–10 minutes, according
to their size and thickness, turning them halfway
through cooking. Serve with the salsa verde.

FRITTO MISTO DI MARE

Deep-fried fish

*This dish, prepared with the catch of the day, was my
favorite Sunday lunch when I was a child in Italy. I
loved the surprise of finding the different types of fish
when I bit into the crispy, olive oil-flavored coating. You
can use larger fish cut into pieces or other shellfish.*

INGREDIENTS

½lb (250g) small squid, prepared (see page 153)
olive oil for deep-frying
½lb (250g) peeled raw shrimp
½lb (250g) small fish
salt and black pepper
flour, to coat the fish
2 lemons, quartered

PREPARATION

1 Cut the squid bodies into rings, leaving the
tentacles whole. Heat plenty of olive oil in a deep
fryer. Season the squid, shrimp, and fish well, then
roll in the flour, shaking off any excess.
2 When the oil is hot enough to crisp a piece of
bread, add the fish in batches and fry until golden.
Drain on paper towels. Serve with lemon quarters.

BOURRIDE

Provençal fish stew

*A rich, creamy broth made with white fish steaks and
thickened with aïoli, a garlicky mayonnaise. Serves 6–8.*

INGREDIENTS

2lb (1kg) fish trimmings
2 carrots, peeled
2 celery ribs, chopped
stalk of 1 fennel bulb
1 onion, peeled
½ cup (125ml) dry vermouth
2 parsley sprigs
piece of orange zest
salt and black pepper
6 plump garlic cloves, peeled
½ tsp salt
6 large egg yolks, at room temperature
1¼ cups (300ml) olive oil
3lb (1.5kg) mixed white fish steaks, such as monkfish,
cod, John Dory, sea bass, sea bream, whiting, turbot
6 slices country-style bread

PREPARATION

1 Prepare the stock. Simmer together the fish
trimmings, 8 cups (2 liters) of water, carrots,
celery, fennel, onion, vermouth, parsley, orange
zest, and seasoning for 30 minutes, then strain.
2 Meanwhile, make the aïoli. Make sure all the
ingredients are at room temperature. Using a
mortar and pestle, pound the garlic and salt until
you have a paste. Add 2 egg yolks and pound again.
3 Next, add just a drop of oil and pound until
amalgamated. Continue adding the oil drop by drop
until you have a thick emulsion – do not rush or it
will curdle. When you have a thick mixture, add the
remaining oil in a thin stream, pounding steadily.
4 Place the fish in a pot over medium heat. Pour
over just enough stock to cover them. Bring to a
slow simmer. Cook for 10–15 minutes, or until
the fish starts to flake.
5 Remove the fish from the stock and transfer to a
low oven to keep warm. Measure out 5 cups
(1.25 liters) of stock and let cool for 5 minutes.
6 Beat the remaining egg yolks into half the aïoli.
Add a ladle of stock to the aïoli and egg mixture,
beat well, then pour in the remaining stock.
7 Pour this mixture into a double boiler and warm
gently, beating constantly, until it has a creamy
consistency. Do not allow it to boil and curdle.
8 Toast the bread and lay a slice in each soup
bowl. Arrange the fish on a serving dish, garnished
with the remaining aïoli. Pour the creamy broth
over the bread and serve.

BOUILLABAISSE
Marseillais fish stew

The people of Marseilles will tell you that it is impossible to make an authentic bouillabaisse outside their city, for you will never find the little rock fish sold in their markets specifically for this classic dish. Do at least try to use a wide variety of fish. Serves 8.
Illustrated on page 95.

INGREDIENTS

5lb (2.5kg) fish (including some rock fish, such as rascasse or scorpion fish, weever fish, star gazer, gurnard, and at least 6 fish of the following types: conger eel, red mullet, monkfish, John Dory, sea bream, whiting
3 onions
3 leeks
2 black peppercorns
2 cups (500ml) dry white wine
½ tsp saffron
1 slightly stale baguette
1 cup (250ml) olive oil
6 garlic cloves, peeled
1½lb (750g) plum tomatoes, peeled
2 cloves
bouquet garni made up of 1 fresh bay leaf, 1 sprig fresh thyme, 2 fennel fronds, and 1 piece of dried orange zest
salt and black pepper
ROUILLE
6 garlic cloves, peeled
½ tsp salt
2–3 small dried red chilies, chopped
2 slices day-old country-style bread, crusts removed
⅔ cup (150ml) olive oil

PREPARATION

1 Remove the heads of the fish and place them in a pan. Add 1 whole onion, a leek, the peppercorns, wine, and 10 cups (2.5 liters) of water. Simmer for 20 minutes, and then strain.
2 Cut the bodies of the larger fish into slices, leaving the smaller rock fish whole. Toast the saffron strands briefly and grind to a powder.
3 To make the rouille, crush the garlic, salt, and chilies together to make a paste. Briefly soak the bread in a little water, squeeze dry, and add to the paste. Pound until amalgamated. Gradually add the oil, drop by drop, so that it is amalgamated (this stage can be done using a food processor, but a mortar and pestle give the best results).
4 Cut the baguette into 1½in (3.5cm) slices and bake in the oven until brown and dry.
5 Finely chop the remaining onions, leeks, and 5 of the garlic cloves. Heat 4 tbsp of the oil in a large pan over low heat and add the onion, leeks, and

garlic. Stew slowly for 5 minutes – the vegetables should soften but not brown.
6 Add the tomatoes and cook slowly for 5 minutes longer, until they have broken down.
7 Meanwhile, bring the strained stock to a boil and add the remaining oil and crushed saffron. Stir in the cloves, bouquet garni, and plenty of seasoning. Boil for 5 minutes to amalgamate the liquid and oil.
8 Add the fish: first firmer fleshed fish, such as conger eel and monkfish, then the slices of fish. After 7–8 minutes add the small fish. Cook for 5 minutes longer at a rapid boil.
9 Check the soup's balance of seasoning and discard the bouquet garni. Remove the fish from the soup with a slotted spoon and place on a warmed platter, then pour the broth into a large tureen (alternatively, you can serve the fish and broth together in individual soup bowls). Serve the toasted pieces of baguette with rouille separately.

COQUILLES ST. JACQUES A LA PROVENÇALE
Scallops with garlic and Cognac

The key to cooking scallops is to do so very quickly so that they remain juicy and tender — as in this simple yet luxurious recipe from the South of France which is a favorite of mine. If you buy scallops in the shell, keep the shells to serve them in.
Illustrated on page 94.

INGREDIENTS

16 large scallops, preferably with corals
salt and black pepper
2 tbsp all-purpose flour
4 tbsp olive oil
4 garlic cloves, very finely chopped
2 tbsp Cognac
¼ cup chopped fresh parsley

PREPARATION

1 Clean the scallops, if necessary (see page 153). Slice the white part of the scallops in half, leaving the corals whole. Season all the pieces well, then sprinkle them with a little flour.
2 Heat the oil in a heavy pan. Scatter in the garlic and when it begins to sizzle put in the white parts of the scallops. Cook for no more than 1 minute.
3 Add the corals and cook for a minute longer, turning the white parts. Stand back, pour in the Cognac and as soon as it sizzles, take the pan off the heat and sprinkle over the parsley. Serve in the scallop shells or on slices of toast.

ROMESCO DE PEIX

Seafood stew with romesco pepper sauce

*This classic dish from Tarragona, the Roman
city on the coast south of Barcelona, takes its name from
the* romesco, *or* nyora, *chili pepper traditionally used.
The romesco sauce in which the fish is cooked is very
garlicky, thick with nuts, and wonderfully aromatic.*

INGREDIENTS

1 large mild dried red chili, preferably romesco
½ cup (60g) blanched hazelnuts
½ cup (60g) blanched almonds
1½lb (750g) mixed whitefish steaks such as monkfish,
sea bass, swordfish, sea bream
salt and black pepper
1 tbsp all-purpose flour, plus flour for dusting
⅓ cup (90ml) olive oil
2 small dried red chilies
1 whole garlic bulb
1 slice white bread, crusts removed
2 tbsp chopped fresh parsley
¾ cup (175ml) dry white wine
2 cups (475ml) fish stock (see page 155)
1lb (500g) clams or mussels

PREPARATION

1 Soak the large chili in warm water for 1 hour.
Toast the nuts in a dry skillet.

2 Cut the fish into 2–3in (5–7cm) pieces, season
well, and dust with flour. Heat 4 tbsp of oil in a
large pan and fry the fish for 5 minutes, turning
halfway through, until golden, then set aside.

3 Drain the romesco pepper and finely chop; chop
the small chilies. Peel all the garlic cloves and set
aside half. Warm the oil in which the fish was fried
and add the chopped chilies and half the garlic. Fry
for 2 minutes.

4 Warm 1 tbsp of oil in a separate skillet and fry
the slice of bread until golden.

5 In a food processor, grind the hazelnuts and
almonds, the romesco and small chilies, the
cooked and raw garlic, bread, parsley, and 4 tbsp
of wine to a paste.

6 Heat the remaining oil in the large pan. Add the
paste and 1 tbsp of flour. Cook gently for
2 minutes, stirring to amalgamate the flour, then
slowly pour in the remaining wine. Finally, add the
fish stock and seasoning. Simmer for 5 minutes,
stirring all the time, until the sauce thickens.
Meanwhile, clean the clams (see page 153).

7 Place the fish steaks and the shellfish in the large
pan, coating them with sauce. Allow to simmer,
uncovered, for 10 minutes, until the fish is tender
and the shellfish have opened. Serve immediately.

Olive oil

Flour

Black pepper

Salt

Almonds

Hazelnuts

Romesco chili

Swordfish

Monkfish

Sea bass

Small dried
chilies

Garlic

White
bread

Parsley

White wine

Fish stock

Clams

ESCABECHE

Fish cooked in aromatic vinegar

The Spanish developed the habit of marinating cooked fish in a vinegary mixture of vegetables to make sure the fish kept on long sea voyages – which may be why versions of this dish turn up in the Caribbean. Serves 6.

INGREDIENTS

salt and black pepper
2lb (1kg) fish fillets, such as sea bream,
sea bass, swordfish, tuna
flour, to dust
½ cup (125ml) olive oil
4 bay leaves
1 lemon, sliced
6 parsley sprigs
2 large onions
6 garlic cloves, peeled
2 large carrots, peeled and thinly sliced
1 tsp sweet paprika
¾ cup (175ml) white vinegar
¾ cup (175ml) white wine

PREPARATION

1 Season the fish well, then dust lightly with flour.
2 Heat the oil and when it is hot, add the fish. Fry for 4 minutes on each side until lightly golden. Remove the fish and place in an earthenware dish. Arrange the bay leaves, lemon, and parsley on top.
3 Peel the onions, cut in half, and slice into fine half-moons. Add the whole garlic cloves, carrot, and onion to the remaining olive oil and fry on low heat for 10 minutes, until the onion is soft.
4 Add the paprika, seasoning, vinegar, and wine and allow to simmer for 5 minutes. Take off the heat, add ⅓ cup (90ml) of water, and let cool.
5 Pour the cooled vinegar and vegetable mixture over the fish and leave for at least 24 hours. The fish will keep for up to a week in the refrigerator but should always be served at room temperature.

USKUMRU DOLMASI

Stuffed mackerel

It is said that the suitability of a Turkish wife was once measured by her ability to stuff a mackerel; whether you are a male or female cook, this is a dish that requires patience. Its feast-day origins are apparent in its richness and I prefer to serve it in small slices as an appetizer for 8 people. You need a needle and thread to sew up the fish after stuffing.

INGREDIENTS

4 small mackerel, ungutted, approximately
12oz (375g) each
2 tbsp olive oil
1 large onion, finely chopped
2 garlic cloves, finely chopped
1 cup (125g) chopped walnuts
½ cup (60g) raisins
1 tsp cinnamon
2 cloves, ground
4 whole allspice, ground
pinch of nutmeg
salt and black pepper
3 tbsp finely chopped fresh parsley
olive, sunflower, or vegetable oil for deep-frying
2 large eggs, beaten
2 cups (175g) dried bread crumbs
4 lemons, quartered

PREPARATION

1 Remove the head of the mackerel. Pull the guts out through the cavity and discard them, taking care not to break the delicate skin.
2 Break the backbone of the mackerel and begin to work loose the flesh, as shown in step 1, opposite. Squeeze out the flesh, leaving the layer attached to the fish skin intact.
3 Warm the olive oil in a heavy skillet over low heat and add the onion and garlic. Stew gently for 10 minutes, until the onion is soft.
4 Stir in the flesh of the fish, the walnuts, raisins, spices, and seasoning to taste. Cook the stuffing gently for 5 minutes longer, stirring continuously. Mix in the parsley and let cool.
5 When the stuffing is cool enough to handle, pack it into the fish skins, following steps 2–3, opposite.
6 Pour oil into a large pan to a depth of 1in (2.5cm) and heat gently.
7 Dip the fish first in the beaten egg and then in the bread crumbs, making sure it is well coated. Fry in the oil for 5 minutes on either side.
8 Cut off the stitched end of the mackerel and discard. Cut the fish into slices and serve hot or cold with lemon wedges.

STUFFING A MACKEREL

1 Bend back the fish at the tail end to break the backbone. Massage the fish with your thumbs to loosen the flesh, pull out the backbone, and carefully squeeze out the flesh, picking out small bones.

2 Using a teaspoon, pack the stuffing into the cavity, pushing it as far down the tail as you can, but leaving a ½in (1cm) space at the head end.

3 Using some strong thread and a darning needle, stitch the two sides of the head cavity together, being careful not to tear the skin.

SARDALYA SARMASI

Stuffed sardines in grape leaves

Turkish cooks have developed the skill of grilling fish over charcoal to something of an art form. But even they find it difficult to prevent sardines from breaking up on the barbecue, so they first wrap the fish in grape leaves. Illustrated on page 94.

INGREDIENTS

8 grape leaves in brine
8 fresh sardines, scaled and gutted (see page 152)
4–6 tbsp finely chopped fresh cilantro
4–6 tbsp finely chopped fresh parsley
4 garlic cloves, crushed and finely chopped
¼ cup (60ml) olive oil
salt and black pepper
2 lemons, quartered, to serve

PREPARATION

1 Soak the grape leaves in water for 45 minutes, changing the water halfway through.
2 With a sharp knife, slit the sardines along the length of the belly. Hold them open, then press them flat and pull out the backbone. Pick over the flesh, removing any stray bones.
3 Combine the remaining ingredients, except the lemons, and stuff the fish with the mixture. Drain the grape leaves and wrap one around each fish.
4 Grill the fish, preferably over hot charcoal, for 3–5 minutes on each side. Serve with lemon.

CALAMARES RELLENOS

Stuffed squid

The shape of the body sac of the squid makes it ideal for stuffing. This Spanish recipe uses a savory mixture of cured ham and rice. The stuffed squid are then gently simmered in a thick tomato sauce until meltingly tender.

INGREDIENTS

16 medium squid
1 cup (175g) long-grain rice, rinsed and drained
⅓ cup (90ml) olive oil
1 Spanish onion, finely chopped
4 garlic cloves, finely chopped
6oz (175g) chunk Serrano ham, finely chopped
2 tbsp chopped fresh parsley
1 tsp sweet paprika
salt and black pepper
1 tbsp tomato paste
1½lb (750g) plum tomatoes, peeled, seeded, and chopped
pinch of sugar
1 thyme sprig
¾ cup (175ml) dry white wine

PREPARATION

1 Clean the squid (see page 153), then finely chop the tentacles, leaving the body whole.
2 Bring a large pan of salted water to a boil and boil the rice for 10 minutes. Drain and rinse well under cold water.
3 Heat half the oil in a skillet and add half the onion and half the garlic. Cook gently for 10 minutes, until the onion is soft. Turn up the heat to medium, add the chopped tentacles, ham, parsley, paprika, and plenty of seasoning. Cook for 2 minutes, stirring all the time. Take off the heat and stir in the cooked rice.
4 Make a tomato sauce by heating 2 tbsp of the remaining oil and gently frying the remainder of the onion and garlic until soft, about 10 minutes. Add the tomato paste, chopped tomatoes, sugar, thyme, and seasoning. Cook for 5 minutes, until the tomatoes have broken down. Add the wine, cover, and simmer for 15 minutes.
5 Preheat the oven to 325°F (160°C). Stuff the squid bodies with the rice and ham mixture, taking care not to overfill them.
6 Heat the remaining oil and gently cook the stuffed squid for 5 minutes, turning once, until they are lightly colored but not browned. Using a slotted spoon, transfer them to an earthenware casserole, pour over the tomato sauce, and cover .
7 Bake the squid in the preheated oven for 1 hour, until very tender. Serve piping hot.

TIAN DE SARDINES

Sardines baked with Swiss chard, spinach, and Parmesan

The tian *is a special earthenware gratin dish used in the region around Nice, and it has lent its name to many recipes. In this version, the bubbling top of Parmesan cheese and green leaves hides a surprise filling of sardines. The Niçois also make this dish with the tiny transparent goby fish, or nounats.*

INGREDIENTS

1½lb (750g) fresh sardines, scaled, gutted, and filleted
1lb (500g) Swiss chard leaves
1½lb (750g) baby spinach leaves
⅓ cup (90ml) olive oil, plus oil to grease
2 garlic cloves
¼ cup (60g) long-grain rice, rinsed and drained
2 tbsp chopped fresh parsley
2 cups (175g) freshly grated Parmesan
salt and black pepper
pinch of nutmeg
4 large eggs, beaten
1 cup (60g) fresh white bread crumbs

PREPARATION

1 If you have to fillet the sardines yourself, follow step 2 of Sardalya Sarmasi, opposite. Do not worry if the fillets do not remain whole. The important thing is to remove all the bones.
2 Wash the Swiss chard and spinach, removing any stalks. Cut the leaves into fine strips and dry well.
3 In a heavy pan over low heat, warm 2 tbsp of oil with a peeled garlic clove. Add the Swiss chard and cook for 5 minutes, until the leaves have wilted and the liquid has evaporated. Set aside the Swiss chard and repeat the process with the spinach, using another 2 tbsp of oil and the second peeled clove of garlic.
4 Bring a large pan of salted water to a boil and cook the rice at a rolling boil for 15 minutes. Rinse under cold water and drain thoroughly.
5 Preheat the oven to 425°F (220°C). Stir the cooked rice, Swiss chard and spinach, the parsley, 1¾ cups (150g) of Parmesan, the seasoning, and nutmeg into the beaten eggs.
6 Oil an earthenware gratin dish and put a 1in (2.5cm) layer of the rice mixture over the bottom. Layer the sardines on top and cover with the remainder of the rice mixture.
7 Mix together the remaining Parmesan and the bread crumbs and sprinkle this mixture over the top. Finally, drizzle the top with olive oil.
8 Bake the tian for 25 minutes, until the surface is browned and the contents bubbling. Serve very hot.

SAMAK CHARMOULA

Marinated and baked fish

There is no set recipe for this Moroccan marinade for fish – every cook has a favorite version. You can vary the spices according to your taste, but the marinade should always be thick with herbs. The marinated fish can then be baked, broiled, or used in tagines.

INGREDIENTS

4 garlic cloves
1 tsp salt
juice of 2 lemons
1½ tbsp ground cumin
1 tbsp sweet paprika
¼ tsp cayenne
½ tsp black pepper
4 tbsp chopped fresh cilantro
4 tbsp chopped fresh parsley
½ cup (125ml) olive oil
1 large fish, such as gray mullet or sea bass, approximately
2½lb (1.25kg), scaled and gutted (see page 152)

PREPARATION

1 Using a mortar and pestle, crush the garlic with the salt. In a food processor, mix the crushed garlic with the remaining ingredients except the oil and the fish, until you have a paste.
2 Begin to add the oil in a slow stream, adding it more quickly once the initial amount of oil has amalgamated with the other ingredients.
3 Pour the mixture into a large pan and warm over low heat for 1 minute to bring out the spicy aromas – do not allow the marinade to boil. Take off the heat and cool.
4 Wash the fish well inside and out. Make 4 deep diagonal slashes on each side of the fish, then place it in an earthenware dish. Pour over the sauce and let marinate for 24 hours.
5 When you are ready to cook, preheat the oven to 350°F (180°C). Cover the marinated fish with foil and bake for 45 minutes. Serve hot.

FISH PLAKI

Baked fish with vegetables

*Though it can be hard these days in the Greek islands
to lay your hands on a large fish, if you do it will
probably have been cooked in this simple style, which is
equally popular in neighboring Turkey.*

INGREDIENTS

4 carrots, peeled
4 celery ribs
1 onion
1 green pepper, cored and seeded
2 large potatoes, peeled
¾ cup (175ml) olive oil
salt and black pepper
1 large fish, such as sea bream, weighing 2½lb (1.25kg)
or 4 small fish, such as small gray mullet, scaled and
gutted (see page 152) or 4 fish steaks
4 garlic cloves, finely chopped
2 tbsp tomato paste
¼ tsp cayenne
1 lemon, sliced, to garnish
parsley sprigs, to garnish

PREPARATION

1 Cut the carrots across into slices ½in (1cm) thick.
Cut the celery into ½in (1cm) pieces. Chop the
onion into quarters and then into fine slices. Cut
the pepper into fine strips. Cut the potatoes across
into slices ½in (1cm) thick. Wash and drain all the
vegetables thoroughly.
2 In a large heavy pan with a lid, gently heat the
oil. Add the vegetables, season well, cover, and
cook over low heat for 30 minutes (they should
be quite soft).
3 Preheat the oven to 400°F (200°C).
4 Remove the vegetables from the oil with a slotted
spoon. Lay the fish in an earthenware dish and
carefully arrange the vegetables around and over it.
5 Fry the garlic for 1 minute in the oil in which
the vegetables were cooked, then add the tomato
paste, salt to taste, and cayenne. Cook for
3 minutes longer, stirring all the time.
6 Carefully pour in 4 cups (1 liter) of water. Bring
to a boil, then pour the liquid over the fish and
vegetables, making sure you scrape all the garlic
out of the pan.
7 Bake the dish uncovered in the oven for
30–45 minutes, depending on the size of fish, until
the fish is very tender (Turkish cooks often prefer
to cook fish longer).
8 Let the fish cool in its liquid and serve at room
temperature, garnished with slices of lemon and
sprigs of parsley.

Olive oil

Potatoes

Green pepper

Onion

Celery

Carrots

Gray mullet

Salt

Black pepper

Garlic

Tomato paste

Cayenne

Lemon

Parsley

MEAT DISHES

Mediterranean cooks are economical by nature: meat is often used in only small quantities to enhance the flavor of vegetable dishes and all parts of the animal are used, with delicious results. Cured meats and sausages play an important role and, in season, game is frequently found on the table. The most commonly offered meats are pork in the west of the region, lamb in the east and poultry throughout. On feast days, meat dishes take center stage – a whole lamb roasted on the spit is a particular specialty.

DJEJ MESHWI

Moroccan grilled spring chicken

Illustrated on page 50.

INGREDIENTS

4 Rock Cornish hens
⅓ cup (90ml) olive oil
juice of 2 lemons
4 garlic cloves, crushed and finely chopped
1 tsp black pepper
sea salt
2 tbsp chopped fresh parsley
2 lemons, quartered, to serve

PREPARATION

1 Split the chickens for grilling (see page 155).
2 Mix together the olive oil, lemon juice, garlic, and pepper and rub this marinade all over the chickens, slipping some between the skin and the flesh. Let the chickens marinate for several hours, turning them frequently.
3 Grill the chickens, preferably over charcoal, skin side down. Cook until the skin is nicely browned, about 10 minutes. Turn the chickens over, sprinkle with plenty of salt, and brush with the marinade. Cook for 10 minutes longer, then turn over again and cook for a final 5 minutes to crisp the skin. Sprinkle with parsley and serve with little bowls of coarse sea salt and lemon quarters.

ŞIŞ KÖFTESI

Turkish ground meat on skewers

Illustrated on page 50.

INGREDIENTS

1 large onion
1½lb (750g) ground lamb, preferably from the shoulder
2 garlic cloves, finely chopped
4 tbsp chopped fresh parsley or coriander
1 tsp sweet paprika
1 tsp ground cumin
pinch of cayenne
1 tsp salt
½ tsp black pepper
2 lemons, quartered, to serve

PREPARATION

1 Grate the onion – be careful to catch the juices.
2 Blend all the ingredients except the lemons in a food processor until you have a smooth paste. Leave the mixture in a bowl for at least 30 minutes for the flavors to mingle.
3 Dampen your hands, take an egg-sized piece of the meat mixture, and fashion it into a long thin sausage shape on the skewer (see page 155). Continue until all the mixture is used.
4 Grill the kebabs, preferably over charcoal, for 6–7 minutes, turning them frequently. Serve hot with lemon quarters.

YOĞURTLU KEBAB

Lamb kebabs with yogurt

This Turkish dish, popular throughout the eastern Mediterranean, adds fresh tomato sauce, yogurt, bread, and pine nuts to smoky morsels of lamb, making them into a complete meal.

INGREDIENTS

1½lb (750g) lamb, preferably from the shoulder, cut into 1in (2.5cm) cubes
3 tbsp olive oil
1½lb (750g) plum tomatoes, peeled, seeded, and chopped
salt and black pepper
pinch of sugar, optional
2 pita or other flat breads
½ pint (300ml) plain yogurt, strained through cheesecloth
2 tbsp pine nuts
1 tsp sweet paprika
1 tbsp chopped fresh parsley, to serve
MARINADE
1 mild onion, grated
juice of 1 lemon
2 tbsp olive oil
2 garlic cloves, crushed
1 tsp ground cumin
½ tsp sweet paprika
1 sprig fresh thyme
salt and black pepper

PREPARATION

1 Mix together all the marinade ingredients and pour over the lamb. Marinate for at least 2 hours, turning the meat once or twice.
2 Heat 1 tbsp of oil in a pan and add the tomato flesh. Cook gently for 10 minutes, stirring frequently, until the tomatoes have broken down and formed a thick sauce. Remove from the heat and season, adding a pinch of sugar if the tomatoes are not sweet enough.
3 Remove the meat from the marinade and thread on skewers. Grill, preferably over charcoal, for a minimum of 4–5 minutes on each side.
4 While the meat is cooking, split the breads in half lengthwise and toast until lightly browned on both sides. Break the toasted bread into squares and scatter over the base of a serving dish. Spread the tomato sauce over the bread.
5 Lay the kebabs on top of the tomato sauce and cover with yogurt. Toast the pine nuts until golden.
6 Warm the remaining oil and stir in the paprika. Pour the oil over the yogurt and scatter the pine nuts and parsley over all.

ŞIŞ KEBAB

Turkish lamb kebabs

Illustrated on page 51.

INGREDIENTS

1½lb (750g) lamb, preferably from the shoulder, cut into 1in (2.5cm) cubes
1 mild onion, grated
juice of 1 lemon
2 tbsp olive oil
2 cloves garlic, crushed
2 bay leaves
salt and black pepper
1 tbsp chopped parsley, to serve

PREPARATION

1 Mix together the onion, lemon juice, olive oil, garlic, bay leaves, and a generous amount of seasoning and pour over the lamb. Marinate for at least 2 hours, turning the meat once or twice.
2 Remove the meat from the marinade and thread on skewers. Grill, preferably over charcoal, for a minimum of 4–5 minutes on each side. Serve scattered with chopped parsley.

PINCHOS MORUNOS

Spanish pork kebabs

Illustrated on page 38.

INGREDIENTS

1¼lb (625g) pork scallops
1 tsp ground cumin
1 tsp sweet paprika
½ tsp cayenne, or more to taste
1 dried bay leaf, crumbled
½ tsp dried thyme
⅓ cup (90ml) olive oil
2 lemons, quartered, and
small bowl of sea salt, to serve

PREPARATION

1 Trim any fat from the pork and cut the meat into ¾in (1.5cm) cubes.
2 Mix together the spices, herbs, and oil to make a marinade and pour it over the pork, making sure every piece is well coated. Let marinate for at least 4 hours, preferably overnight.
3 Thread 2 or 3 cubes on small skewers. Cook over charcoal or under a medium broiler for 8–10 minutes, turning the kebabs and basting frequently with the marinade. Serve with lemon quarters and sea salt.

FOIE DE VEAU AUX CÂPRES

Calf's liver in tomato sauce with capers

Much of the cooking of the Mediterranean has a rough-and-ready feel, but this is undeniably a luxury dish. Thin slices of calf's liver just seared in the pan, then bathed in a deep red tomato sauce flecked with the green of capers and parsley, are a favorite in Provence.

INGREDIENTS

¾lb (375g) calf's liver, cut into very thin slices
1 tbsp olive oil
1 tbsp chopped fresh parsley
TOMATO AND CAPER SAUCE
2 tbsp extra-virgin olive oil
1½lb (750g) juicy plum tomatoes, peeled and chopped
1 tsp tomato paste
pinch of sugar
salt and black pepper
1 cup (250ml) dry white wine
2 tbsp capers, rinsed and drained

PREPARATION

1 First make the sauce. Heat the extra-virgin olive oil in a heavy pan and add the tomatoes, tomato paste, sugar, and seasoning. Cook over low heat for 10 minutes, stirring frequently, until the tomatoes have broken down.
2 Add the wine, bring to a boil, and turn down to a simmer. Let simmer uncovered for 30 minutes, until you have a thick sauce.
3 Add the capers to the tomato sauce and check for seasoning – it should be quite peppery with plenty of bite.
4 To cook the liver, choose a large pan in which all the slices will lie flat. Heat the olive oil over high heat, and when it is hot but not smoking, add the liver. If the liver is cut thin enough, it should need no more than 30 seconds' cooking on each side.
5 Transfer the liver to a warmed serving plate. Pour the tomato sauce into the pan in which the liver was cooked and swirl it around to incorporate the oil. Pour the sauce over the liver, sprinkle with parsley, and serve.

RIÑONES AL JEREZ

Kidneys cooked in sherry

In Spain this dish is often prepared using veal kidneys, but the much smaller lamb kidneys are a good substitute. Riñones al Jerez can be served as part of a selection of tapas, but the proportions given here are for a quickly prepared main course, to be served with rice and a green salad.

INGREDIENTS

2 tbsp olive oil
12 lamb kidneys, washed, cored, and quartered
2 garlic cloves, finely chopped
⅔ cup (150ml) fino sherry
salt and black pepper

PREPARATION

1 Heat the oil in a heavy pan over high heat. When the oil is very hot, add the kidneys and garlic and cook for 2 minutes, stirring continuously.
2 Stand back and add the sherry – be careful; it will spatter. Season and cook over high heat for a minute longer. Serve immediately.

LA PIZZAIOLA

Steak with tomato sauce

Few recipes could be simpler than the pizzaiola of southern Italy, yet have such dramatic results. In minutes a potentially disappointing steak can be transformed into a dish redolent with the Mediterranean flavors of olive oil, tomatoes, herbs, and garlic.

INGREDIENTS

salt and black pepper
4 thinly cut steaks, each weighing 4–5oz (125–150g)
3 tbsp olive oil
3 garlic cloves
4 ripe plum tomatoes, peeled, seeded, and chopped or
14oz (425g) can whole peeled tomatoes, chopped
2 tsp chopped fresh oregano or ½ tsp dried

PREPARATION

1 Season the steaks well. Heat the oil in a heavy skillet until it is hot but not smoking. Add the steaks and cook for 30 seconds on each side to sear them. Remove the steaks from the oil and set aside.
2 Add the garlic to the oil in the skillet, and as soon as it starts to sizzle, add the tomatoes, oregano, and a good grinding of salt and pepper. Simmer for 5 minutes, stirring frequently.
3 Return the steaks to the skillet and cook them for 5 minutes, turning them once.

SOUMANATE BI' LEINAB

Quail with grapes

This elegant recipe from Morocco is a simple but delicious way to prepare quail. It is best made with slightly underripe green grapes. Similar recipes for partridges are found over the water in Andalusia.

INGREDIENTS

4 tbsp butter
8 quail
12oz (375g) seedless green grapes
salt and black pepper
1 tsp ground ginger

PREPARATION

1 Melt the butter over low heat in a heavy skillet just large enough to hold all the birds lying flat. Add the quail and cook for 10 minutes, turning frequently, until they are lightly browned.
2 Meanwhile, purée three quarters of the grapes in a food processor. Press the resulting pulp through a sieve, reserving the juice.
3 Season the quail and sprinkle with ginger. Add the grape juice, turn the quail breast side down, cover, and let cook over low heat for 10 minutes.
4 Slice the remaining grapes in half and add to the pan. Turn the birds breast side up and cook for 3–4 minutes longer, until the grapes are warmed through. Serve immediately.

ALBONDIGAS

Pork and parsley meatballs

Fried balls of ground pork studded with parsley and flavored with garlic and spices are a favorite tapa *in Spain. Served with a fresh tomato sauce, they also make a delicious main course.*

INGREDIENTS

1 small onion
1lb (500g) finely ground pork, preferably from the loin
1 cup (60g) white bread crumbs
1 cup (60g) finely chopped fresh parsley
2 garlic cloves, minced
1 tsp sweet paprika
pinch of freshly grated nutmeg
pinch of cayenne
2 large eggs
salt and black pepper
sunflower or vegetable oil for frying
flour, to dust

PREPARATION

1 Mince the onion, being careful to catch the juices. Mix together the pork, onion, bread crumbs, parsley, garlic, paprika, nutmeg, cayenne, 1 egg, and plenty of seasoning. Break off walnut-sized pieces and shape into balls.
2 Pour oil to a depth of ½in (1cm) into a skillet and warm over medium heat.
3 Roll the meatballs in seasoned flour. Beat the remaining egg. When the oil is nearly smoking, dip each ball into the egg and then lower it into the hot oil to seal it. Reduce the heat and let cook for 10 minutes.
4 Turn the meatballs over and cook slowly for another 10 minutes, or until they are cooked through. Turn up the heat at the end of cooking to crisp them – they should be golden.
5 Drain the meatballs on paper towels and serve hot or cold with Allioli (see page 66).

DAOUD PASHA

Spicy lamb meatballs with pine nuts in tomato sauce

Meatballs cooked over charcoal or poached in a sauce are a distinctive feature of the cooking of the eastern Mediterranean. In this Syrian dish they are studded with pine nuts and cooked in a lemon-sharp tomato sauce.

INGREDIENTS

¼ tsp ground cumin
¼ tsp ground cinnamon
¼ tsp ground coriander
½ tsp black pepper
¼ cup (60g) pine nuts
1¼lb (625g) finely ground lamb
2 onions
2 tbsp olive oil
¼ cup (60g) tomato paste
juice of 1 lemon
salt
2 tbsp chopped fresh parsley or cilantro

PREPARATION

1 Mix the spices and pine nuts into the lamb. Break off walnut-sized pieces and shape into balls.
2 Peel the onions, cut in half, and slice into fine half-moons. Choose a large deep skillet and slowly heat the oil. Add the onion and cook gently for 20 minutes over low heat, stirring occasionally. The onion should be soft but not colored.
3 Add the meatballs to the pan and cook gently, shaking the pan occasionally. After 5 minutes the meatballs should be lightly colored all over.
4 Beat together the tomato paste and lemon juice and add sufficient water to make 2 cups (500ml). Pour this mixture into the pan, add salt to taste, and let simmer for 20 minutes, turning the meatballs halfway through cooking.
5 Check the seasoning of the sauce, sprinkle the dish with parsley, and serve hot.

ARNI FRIKASE AVGOLEMONO

Fricassee of lamb with egg and lemon sauce

Avgolemono, the sharp egg and lemon sauce beloved of the Greeks, marries especially well with their favorite meat, lamb. Traditionally the meat is slowly stewed before the final addition of the sauce, but I find this quick version very satisfactory for a simple summer lunch. Illustrated on page 112.

INGREDIENTS

1¼lb (625g) boneless lamb stew meat
salt and black pepper
1 bunch scallions
1 head romaine lettuce
2 tbsp olive oil
1½ cups (350ml) light lamb stock (see page 155)
3 egg yolks
juice of 2 lemons
1 tbsp chopped fresh dill

PREPARATION

1 Cut the lamb into bite-sized pieces, approximately 1in (2.5cm) square, trimming off any fat. Season the chunks of meat well.
2 Roughly chop the scallions, including the green part. Remove the heart of the lettuce, discarding the large outer leaves. Wash the heart well and chop into ½in (1cm) wide strips.
3 Heat the oil in a large skillet over medium heat. Add the scallions and lamb and cook for 2 minutes, turning the meat frequently until it is browned all over.
4 Add the lettuce and the lamb stock, bring rapidly to a boil, then reduce the heat to low. Simmer gently for 5 minutes.
5 Meanwhile, beat the egg yolks with the lemon juice in a bowl. After the stock has simmered for 5 minutes, drain off the hot liquid from the skillet and pour it into the egg and lemon mixture, whisking all the time to prevent the egg from curdling. Put the lamb and lettuce in a serving dish and keep warm in a low oven.
6 Turn the heat down as low as it will go and return the liquid to the skillet. Simmer for 2–3 minutes, whisking continuously, until the sauce thickens slightly – do not allow the liquid to return to a boil or it will curdle.
7 Take the skillet off the heat, stir in the dill, and add more seasoning to taste. Pour the sauce over the lamb and lettuce. Serve immediately.

POULET SAUTE AUX HERBES DE PROVENCE

Chicken sautéed with herbs and garlic in white wine

As this dish cooks, it gives off those aromas that remind me of the Mediterranean – pungent garlic in fruity olive oil, the fragrance of herbs, and the headiness of wine. This is a basic recipe for chicken, but you'll find plenty of regional variations. Accompany with a green salad. Illustrated on page 112.

INGREDIENTS

3 plump garlic cloves
2 tbsp olive oil
1 chicken, cut up, (see page 154) or 8 chicken thighs
and drumsticks
a few sprigs each of fresh thyme, oregano, and rosemary
1 cup (250ml) dry white wine
salt and black pepper
juice of ½ lemon

PREPARATION

1 Peel the garlic and chop the cloves into quarters.
2 Heat the oil in a deep heavy skillet large enough to take all the chicken pieces. Add the chicken, garlic, and herbs and cook briskly for 5 minutes, turning the chicken to brown it lightly all over.
3 Pour in the wine, bring to a boil, and turn down to a simmer. Add seasoning, cover, and let cook for 30 minutes, turning the chicken pieces halfway through cooking.
4 Finish with the lemon juice and serve very hot. The chicken should be tender and the sauce syrupy.

ARNI FRIKASE AVGOLEMONO
*Fricassee of lamb with egg
and lemon sauce
(page 111)*

ARROSTA DI MAIALE
Roast pork Italian style
(page 114)

POULET SAUTE AUX HERBES DE PROVENCE
Chicken sautéed with herbs and garlic
in white wine
(page 111)

MOUSSAKA

Baked eggplant layered with lamb

Most moussakas served today are quite unlike the Greek original, with its plump eggplant, spiced lamb in a rich sauce, and light cheese custard, layered and baked until the flavors meld. Served with bread and a green salad, it is a satisfying meal. Serves 6–8.

INGREDIENTS

2lb (1kg) eggplant
salt
2 white onions, finely chopped
olive oil for frying
1½lb (750g) ground lamb
1 tsp ground cinnamon
1 tsp ground allspice
black pepper
1 cup (250ml) red wine
2lb (1kg) plum tomatoes, peeled, seeded, and chopped
1 tsp tomato paste
1 tsp honey
4 tbsp chopped fresh parsley
1 tbsp dried oregano
½ cup (125ml) lamb or chicken stock (see page 155)
2 cups (500ml) whole milk
½ cup (125g) cottage cheese
⅓ cup (90g) feta cheese
3 large whole eggs, plus 3 egg yolks
pinch of freshly grated nutmeg
1 cup (60g) white bread crumbs
½ cup (60g) freshly grated Greek hard cheese or Parmesan

PREPARATION

1 Wash the eggplant and cut into ¼in (5mm) slices. Salt and blot them (see page 150).
2 Stew the onion gently in 3 tbsp of oil for 15 minutes, until soft but not browned. Turn up the heat and add the lamb, spices, and seasoning. Cook over high heat for 5 minutes, stirring continuously, until the meat is browned all over.
3 Pour in the wine and allow to bubble for 5 minutes. Add the tomatoes, tomato paste, and honey, turn down to a simmer, and let cook uncovered for 10 minutes, stirring occasionally to help the tomatoes break down.
4 Add the herbs and stock, and simmer gently for 30 minutes, until the sauce is very thick.
5 Process or beat together the milk and cottage and feta cheeses. Add the eggs and egg yolks, and beat well. Stir in the nutmeg.
6 Heat this mixture in a double boiler over gently simmering water for 15–20 minutes, stirring continuously, until the custard thickens – do not allow it to boil or it will curdle.
7 Pour just enough oil into a nonstick skillet to cover the bottom and place over medium heat. When the oil is very hot, add the rinsed and dried eggplant slices. Cook for 1 minute on each side, then drain on paper towels. Repeat, adding more oil if necessary, until all the eggplant is cooked.
8 Preheat the oven to 350°F (180°C). Choose a large deep baking dish. Assemble the moussaka, starting with a layer of eggplant, following with lamb, cheese custard, more eggplant, lamb, eggplant again, and finishing with cheese custard.
9 Mix together the bread crumbs and grated cheese and sprinkle over the top. Bake for 1 hour, until the top is crispy and the contents bubbling.

ARROSTA DI MAIALE

Roast pork Italian style

The Italian love affair with pork reaches its height with porchetta, roast stuffed suckling pig. Fennel is an essential ingredient of its stuffing, and it is also used with smaller roasts, as here. The use of wine ensures moist meat. Serves 6. Illustrated on page 113.

INGREDIENTS

3 garlic cloves
salt
3 fennel bulbs, fronds attached
½ tsp fennel seeds
4 tbsp olive oil
1 bottle white wine (approximately)
3–3½lb (1.5–1.75kg) pork roast, on the bone
black pepper
1 rosemary sprig
⅓ cup (90ml) marsala wine, optional

PREPARATION

1 Preheat the oven to 350°F (180°C).
2 Crush the garlic cloves with a little salt. Remove the fennel fronds and chop roughly. Using a food processor, process the garlic, fennel seeds and fronds, oil, and ½ cup (125ml) wine to make a paste.
3 Make incisions in the pork and smear with paste. Season with pepper and place in a small roasting pan. Surround with halved fennel bulbs. Pour in wine to a depth of ¾in (1.5cm). Add the rosemary and cook for 30 minutes.
4 Reduce the heat to 325°F (160°C) and cook for 2–2½ hours, basting with the pan juices.
5 Remove the pork and fennel and let sit for 10 minutes. Skim the fat from the pan.
6 Add the marsala or a glass of the remaining wine to the pan. Place over high heat, reduce to a syrupy sauce, and pour over the pork.

PATO A LA SEVILLANA

Duck with olives, orange, and sherry

This recipe brings together three of the culinary treasures
of Andalusia – the bone-dry sherry, with its tang of
salt, green olives, and sweet, juicy oranges.

INGREDIENTS

1 duck, weighing 4lb (2kg)
2 oranges
3 garlic cloves
1 onion, chopped
1 carrot, chopped
1 cup (125g) green olives
1 cup (250ml) fino sherry
4 peppercorns
2 bay leaves
2 fresh thyme sprigs
salt and black pepper

PREPARATION

1 Preheat the oven to 325°F (180°C).
2 Prick the duck all over with a fork. Place 1
orange, cut in half, and 1 unpeeled garlic clove
inside the bird. Roast the bird breast side down on
a wire rack over a pan for 30 minutes.
3 After the duck has cooked for 30 minutes, drain
off the fat. Turn it breast side up and roast for
15 minutes longer.
4 Meanwhile, gently cook the onion, carrot, and
remaining garlic, finely chopped, in a tablespoon
of the reserved duck fat for 20 minutes, until very
soft. Add 1½ cups (350ml) of water and simmer for
30 minutes to make a stock. Add the olives to the
stock for the last 5 minutes.
5 Remove the duck from the oven and cut into
4 pieces. Place the duck in a casserole. Pour over
the contents of the stock pan and the juice of the
remaining orange. Add the peppercorns, bay
leaves, thyme, and seasoning.
6 Bring to a boil, turn down to a simmer, cover,
and cook on low heat for 45 minutes. Remove the
thyme before serving.

CAPRIOLO IN AGRODOLCE

Venison in a sweet and sour sauce

The ancient Romans were very fond of sauces made with
honey and vinegar; the chocolate in this sauce is a later
addition. Hare and wild boar are also cooked in this way.

INGREDIENTS

1½lb (750g) venison steak or stew meat
1 large onion, chopped
2 large carrots, chopped
2 ribs celery, chopped
4 garlic cloves, peeled and crushed
bouquet garni made up of 1 fresh bay leaf and 2 sprigs
each of fresh rosemary and thyme
black pepper
6 juniper berries
¼ cup (60ml) olive oil
⅔ cup (150ml) red wine vinegar
1¼ cups (300ml) red wine
salt
flour, to dust
2oz (60g) unsweetened chocolate, grated
1 tbsp honey
2 tbsp chopped fresh parsley

PREPARATION

1 Trim the venison and cut into large pieces.
2 Place the pieces of venison in a bowl with the
onion, carrots, and celery. Add the garlic and
bouquet garni, plenty of pepper, and the juniper
berries. Pour over half the oil, 2 tbsp of vinegar,
and all the wine. Marinate for at least 4 hours,
preferably overnight.
3 Preheat the oven to 275°F (140°C), if using (see
step 5). Remove the venison from the marinade and
pat dry. Season the flour and dust the venison.
Heat the remaining oil in a pan and brown the meat.
4 Remove the meat from the pan and set aside.
Strain the vegetable marinade, reserving the liquid,
and heat the vegetables in the pan for 5 minutes.
5 Bring the marinade to a boil in a small pan. Add
the chocolate, stirring to melt it. Return the meat
to the pan, pour over the hot marinade and, if
necessary, enough water to cover it. Cover the pan
with aluminum foil and then with the lid. Place
over a very low heat, so that the liquid is barely
simmering, and cook for 2½–3 hours. Alternatively,
cook in the preheated oven for 3 hours.
6 Just before serving, make a syrup by mixing the
honey with 2 tbsp of water over low heat. Stir in
the remaining vinegar and allow to simmer for
2 minutes. Add this mixture to the pan.
7 Check the seasoning and balance of flavor – add
more vinegar, if desired – then sprinkle with parsley.

DAUBE DE BOEUF
Beef casserole

This classic Provençal dish is not for a cook in a hurry. Traditionally the daube was left to simmer on the stove all day, so that by evening the kitchen would be filled with the powerful scent of wine and herbs. The slower and longer the dish cooks, the better it will taste. You can, if you like, cut down the marinating time, although the flavor will not be as intense. Daube tastes even better if made a day in advance. Serves 6–8.

INGREDIENTS

3lb (1.5kg) beef shank steaks or chuck
2 onions, quartered
3 garlic cloves, peeled and crushed
black pepper
pinch of ground allspice
large bouquet garni made up of 4 sprigs each of fresh thyme and rosemary, 1 bay leaf, and orange zest
2½ cups (600ml) robust red wine
2 tbsp olive oil
8oz (250g) salt pork
6 slices cured bacon or 2 pieces pork rind
2 large carrots, thickly sliced
1lb (500g) plum tomatoes, peeled and quartered
1 cup (125g) small black olives, preferably niçoise
1 cup (60g) dried cèpes or 3 cups (250g) fresh wild mushrooms
salt
1–1½lb (500–750g) fresh noodles, such as tagliatelle

PREPARATION

1 The day before you want to cook the daube, trim the fat from the beef and discard. Cut the meat into large pieces and place in a bowl with the onions, garlic, spices, bouquet garni, wine, and oil. Leave to marinate, preferably for 24 hours.
2 The next day, cut the salt pork into lardons. Place in a large pan together with the bacon slices and cover with water. Bring slowly to a boil and boil for 5 minutes. Drain.
3 Line the base of an earthenware or cast-iron pot with half the bacon or one piece of pork rind.
4 Drain the beef, reserving the marinade. Place the beef, onion, garlic, bouquet garni, and lardons in the pan, interspersing with carrots and tomatoes.
5 Bring the marinade to a boil and pour it over the meat. Lay the remaining bacon or pork rind over the beef. Cover the pan with aluminum foil and then with the lid.
6 Cook the daube for 3½–4 hours, either gently simmering on the stove or in an oven preheated to 275°F (140°C). Meanwhile, blanch the olives for 2 minutes in boiling water. Soak the cèpes in warm water for 15 minutes, then drain.
7 After the daube has cooked for 3 hours, add the olives and cèpes. Replace the lid, and cook for 30 minutes longer, until the meat is thoroughly tender.
8 Just before serving, bring 4 quarts (4 liters) of salted water to a boil and add the noodles. Cook until *al dente*, then drain.
9 Skim the surface fat from the daube, discard the bacon, and check for salt. Serve with the noodles.

Beef shank

Bacon

Salt pork

Onions

Garlic

Black pepper

Ground allspice

Bouquet garni

Red wine

Olive oil

Noodles

Carrots

Tomatoes

Niçoise olives

Dried cèpes

Salt

117

TAGINE D'AGNEAU AUX ABRICOTS

Moroccan casserole of lamb with apricots

Tagines often contain dried or fresh fruit, and those with quince or apricots are my favorites. This rich lamb tagine is delicious accompanied by bread to mop up the fragrant juices. Serves 4–6.

INGREDIENTS

2lb (1kg) boneless shoulder of lamb
2 large onions
1 tsp ground ginger
½ tsp black pepper
½ tsp ground cinnamon
large pinch of saffron
3 tbsp butter
salt
1 bunch cilantro
1 cup (250g) dried apricots

PREPARATION

1 Trim the meat of all fat and cut into large bite-sized pieces. Place the meat in a heavy casserole.
2 Grate one of the onions, being careful to catch the juices, and add to the casserole along with the spices, butter, a large pinch of salt, and half the cilantro tied in a bunch. Pour over 2 cups (500ml) of water, bring to a boil, then turn down to a simmer, and cook for 1 hour.
3 If the dried apricots are plump and moist, there is no need to soak them. Other varieties should be soaked for 1 hour in a little hot water, and then drained before use.
4 Finely chop the remaining onion. Remove the stalks from the rest of the cilantro and roughly chop the leaves. After an hour add these to the casserole and cook for 30 minutes longer.
5 Add the apricots to the casserole and cook for 15–20 minutes, until they have plumped up. Check the seasoning and serve.

OSSO BUCO

Stewed shin of veal

This famous dish is from the north of Italy, the cattle-raising country, though the treatment of the main ingredient has distinctly southern influences. The final spiking with the gremolada, *a mix of lemon, herbs, and garlic, gives the dish enough bite to cheer up the grayest Milanese day.*

INGREDIENTS

2–2½lb (1–1.25kg) veal shanks,
in 4 thick slices with marrow bone
salt and black pepper
flour, to dust
2 tbsp olive oil
2 tbsp butter
2 large carrots, roughly chopped
2 onions, roughly chopped
4 ribs celery, roughly chopped
1½lb (750g) plum tomatoes, peeled, seeded, and chopped
1¼ cups (300ml) dry white wine
1¼ cups (300ml) veal or light beef stock (see page 155)
2 tsp tomato paste
bouquet garni made up of 1 fresh bay leaf and 2 sprigs each of fresh thyme, parsley, rosemary, and a piece of lemon zest

GREMOLADA

zest of ½ lemon
2 garlic cloves, very finely chopped
2 tbsp chopped fresh parsley
2 sage leaves, finely chopped
½ tsp finely chopped rosemary needles

PREPARATION

1 Lightly dust the pieces of veal with seasoned flour. Heat the oil and butter in a pan in which all the slices will fit upright and briefly cook the veal until lightly browned on all sides.
2 Remove the meat from the pan and add the carrot, onion, and celery. Cook gently in the fat until soft but not colored. Return the meat to the pan, upright, and pour over the chopped tomatoes. Preheat the oven to 300°F (150°C).
3 Mix together the wine, stock, and tomato paste in a separate saucepan and bring to a boil. Pour this hot mixture over the veal. Add seasoning and tuck in the bouquet garni. Cover the pan and cook in the preheated oven for 2½–3 hours, until the veal is very tender.
4 Meanwhile, make the gremolada. Finely grate the lemon zest and mix together with the garlic, parsley, sage, and rosemary. Stir this mixture into the dish 5 minutes before serving.

CASSOULET

White beans cooked with pork and duck

This peasant dish from the Languedoc gains its distinctive flavor from the use of goose or duck confit. Serves 6–8.

INGREDIENTS

2½ cups (500g) dried white beans, soaked overnight
bouquet garni made up of 1 fresh bay leaf and 2 sprigs each of fresh parsley, rosemary, thyme, and fennel
3 onions
4 cloves
2 carrots, peeled and halved
5 garlic cloves
8 black peppercorns
8oz (250g) slab bacon
4oz (125g) piece of pancetta or petit salé (see page 22)
4 pieces confit de canard (duck) or confit d'oie (goose) or ½ large duck
2 tbsp olive oil
1lb (500g) Toulouse sausages or other pork sausages
1lb (500g) chorizo or dried garlic sausages
1lb (500g) plum tomatoes, peeled, seeded, and chopped
salt and black pepper

PREPARATION

1 Put the beans in a large heavy pot and cover with 10 cups (2.5 liters) of water. Add the bouquet garni, an onion studded with the cloves, the carrots, 2 garlic cloves, and the peppercorns.
2 Tie the bacon into a tight ball and add to the pan with the pancetta. Bring to a boil and skim off any scum. Reduce the heat, cover, and simmer until the beans are soft but still whole, 1–1½ hours.
3 Meanwhile, gently heat the pieces of confit in a heavy pan to release the fat. Alternatively, if using half a duck, prick the skin all over and then cook the pieces over low heat, skin side down, until the fat is rendered. In each instance, drain off and reserve the fat. Set aside the pieces of duck or goose.
4 Heat the oil in a skillet and finely chop the remaining onions and garlic. Cook for 10 minutes, then remove with a slotted spoon and set aside.
5 Preheat the oven to 275°F (140°C). Drain the beans and remove the bouquet garni, clove-studded onion, garlic, slab of bacon, and pancetta.
6 Take an earthenware casserole and fill it with layers of beans, onion, confit, sausages, and tomatoes, seasoning as you go. Finish with beans.
7 Cook the cassoulet in the preheated oven for 2 hours, then dot with the reserved duck or goose fat. Increase the heat to 350°F (180°C) and remove the lid. When the cassoulet has formed a crust, about 30 minutes, stir this back into the beans, then cook for a final 30 minutes.

PASTA, RICE, AND GRAINS

B read is a central element of the daily diet; no meal is complete without it. Then there are the myriad grain and pasta dishes: the bulgur wheat and couscous of the eastern Mediterranean and North Africa respectively; pilafs, paellas, and risottos; pasta soups and baked pastas. Nor is pasta confined to Italy – there are versions in Provence, Catalonia, and Turkey. These staples of the Mediterranean kitchen are not only nutritionally rich, they are also highly versatile foods that star in both simple everyday meals and some of the most sumptuous classics of the region.

BRUSCHETTA

Garlic bread

Though bruschetta is now interpreted as being bread topped with just about anything that takes the cook's fancy, in its original form it is simply garlic bread. Not just any garlic bread, though – it should be slices of the best country bread, rubbed with juicy garlic, sprinkled with salt and pepper, and drizzled with the best fruity green olive oil.

INGREDIENTS

*4 thick slices country-style Italian bread, preferably whole-wheat sourdough bread
4 plump garlic cloves, peeled and halved
extra-virgin olive oil
salt and black pepper*

PREPARATION

1 Grill the bread slices lightly on both sides (traditionally it is cooked over a wood-burning fire to give it a smoky flavor). Alternatively, bake it in a medium oven until crisp.
2 Rub one side of each slice of bread with the cut side of the garlic pieces.
3 Lay the bread on serving plates and dribble over a generous amount of olive oil. There should be just enough to soak through the bread. Season well and serve immediately.

PANZANELLA

Bread and tomato salad

In Catalonia they rub ripe tomatoes on bread and call it Pa amb Tomàquet. In southern Italy they go further and make a bread and tomato salad, as here. For best results, the tomatoes should have ripened in the sun.

INGREDIENTS

*4 thick slices slightly stale country-style bread
1½lb (750g) very ripe tomatoes
¼ tsp dried oregano
salt
best quality extra-virgin olive oil*

PREPARATION

1 Preheat the oven to 300°F (150°C).
2 Lay the bread on a baking sheet and bake for 15 minutes – the bread should be dry and crisp but not colored.
3 Break the toasted bread into chunks and briefly dampen it under running water, being careful not to soak it. Squeeze it dry with your hands.
4 Place the bread in the bottom of a serving bowl. If the tomatoes are sufficiently ripe, you should be able to squeeze them over the bread, so that the juice and flesh come out, leaving the skin, which should be discarded. Alternatively, peel and chop the tomatoes and scatter over the bread.
5 Sprinkle the salad with oregano and a generous helping of salt. Drizzle with olive oil and let stand for 20 minutes before serving.

VARIATION

• Add extra ingredients such as red onion, olives, cucumber, mozzarella, or anchovies. Replace the dried oregano with fresh oregano, basil, or parsley.

PIZZA ALLA MARINARA
Pizza with tomato sauce

The Neapolitans, who invented the dish, say that pizzas must be cooked in a wood-fired oven. This method may produce an incomparable flavor, but home-cooked pizzas can still be good. This is the original version, with a simple tomato sauce. Makes 2 large pizzas.

INGREDIENTS

DOUGH

1 tsp sugar
2 tbsp active dry yeast
½ tsp salt
3 tbsp olive oil, plus oil for sprinkling
5 cups (625g) all-purpose flour, plus flour to dust

TOMATO SAUCE

¼ cup (60ml) olive oil, plus oil for baking sheet
4 garlic cloves, finely chopped
2lb (1kg) very ripe plum tomatoes, peeled, seeded, and chopped
salt
2 tsp dried oregano
black pepper

PREPARATION

1 Beat the sugar into 1¼ cups (300ml) warm water until it dissolves. Whisk in the yeast. Cover with plastic wrap and leave for 15 minutes, until frothy.
2 Stir the salt and olive oil into the yeast mixture. Pour the flour onto a board and make a well in its center. Gradually add the yeast mixture, working with your hands to incorporate it. When all the liquid has been absorbed, knead the dough until it is smooth and pliable (see page 151).
3 Place the dough in a lightly floured bowl and sprinkle a little oil over the surface. Cover with a clean dish towel and leave in a warm place for 1 hour, or until doubled in volume.
4 Make the tomato sauce. Heat 3 tbsp of oil in a pan and add the garlic. As soon as it starts to sizzle, add the tomatoes. Simmer, uncovered, for 15–20 minutes, stirring frequently. The sauce should be thick and garlicky. Add salt to taste.
5 Preheat the oven to 475°F (240°C). Punch down the dough (see page 151) and divide it in half. Oil a baking sheet and thinly spread half the dough across it with your hands, leaving the edges slightly raised.
6 Spread the base with half the sauce, sprinkle with half the oregano and plenty of pepper, then drizzle over 1 tbsp of olive oil. Repeat with the remaining dough and sauce.
7 Bake at the top of the oven for 12–15 minutes, until the edges of the pizza are crisp. Eat very hot.

FATTOUSH
Lebanese bread salad

This salad has a base of flatbread soaked in vegetable juices and a lemony dressing that makes it substantial and refreshing. As with many eastern Mediterranean salads, plenty of herbs are used. If you can find purslane in the summer, do include it for an authentic flavor – it is easily recognizable from its fleshy stalks.

INGREDIENTS

½ cucumber
1 bunch scallions
1lb (500g) ripe tomatoes, peeled and chopped
salt
1 large flatbread or 2 pita breads
1 romaine lettuce heart
1 large bunch fresh parsley
1 large bunch fresh mint
1 large bunch purslane, optional
⅔ cup (150ml) extra-virgin olive oil
½ cup (125ml) fresh lemon juice
black pepper

PREPARATION

1 Peel the cucumber and dice the flesh. Chop the scallions, including the green tops, into thin slices and mix with the tomatoes and cucumber. Sprinkle with salt and let stand for 10 minutes.
2 Toast the bread until lightly browned. Break it into 1in (2.5cm) squares and scatter them over the base of a serving dish. Cover with the tomato mixture, making sure you pour in all the juices. Let stand for 10 minutes longer, for the bread to absorb the juices.
3 Roughly chop the lettuce, parsley, and mint, discarding large stalks. Strip the purslane leaves from the stalk, if using. Mix the herbs into the salad.
4 Whisk together the oil and lemon juice until the mixture emulsifies, then season with pepper. Pour this dressing over the salad, and serve.

COCA MALLORQUINA

Majorcan-style pizza

*Perhaps more like the Pissaladière (see page 48) than the
Italian pizza, a coca is a slowly cooked bread-based tart.
Ham or sausage can be added to the vegetable topping.*

INGREDIENTS

DOUGH

1 tsp sugar
2 tbsp active dry yeast
2½ cups (300g) unbleached all purpose flour
½ tsp salt
2 tbsp vegetable shortening, cut into small pieces
1 tbsp olive oil

TOPPING

3 small white onions
3 green peppers, cored, seeded, and thinly sliced
2 large tomatoes, thinly sliced
3 garlic cloves, finely chopped
2 tbsp chopped fresh parsley
2 tsp sweet paprika
salt and black pepper
¼ cup (60ml) olive oil

PREPARATION

1 Mix the sugar with ⅔ cup (150ml) warm water,
then beat in the yeast. Cover with plastic wrap and
leave in a warm place for 15 minutes, until frothy.
2 Sift the flour with the salt in a bowl. Crumble
the vegetable shortening into the flour. Add the oil
and rub it into the flour with the shortening.
3 Make a well in the center of the flour mixture
and pour in the yeast solution. Mix quickly with
your hands until you have a smooth, pliable dough
(see page 151). Knead briefly, then place in a bowl,
cover with a clean dish towel, and leave in a warm
place for 1 hour, or until doubled in volume.
4 Meanwhile, peel the onions, cut in half, and slice
into fine half-moons. Mix them with the peppers,
tomatoes, garlic, parsley, and paprika. Season well.
5 Punch down the dough (see page 151) and
knead again. Preheat the oven to 350°F (180°C).
Oil a 12in (30cm) round shallow baking pan.
6 Stretch out the dough to fill the pan, making a
raised edge. Pile on the topping and sprinkle with oil.
7 Bake for 1 hour, until the vegetables are soft and
lightly browned on top and the rim of the dough is
crisp. Serve warm, not piping hot.

PASTA CON LE SARDE

Pasta with sardines

This ancient Sicilian dish gets its unusual flavor from the wild fennel stalks that infuse the water in which the pasta is cooked. If you can't find wild fennel, substitute the stalks, feathery fronds, and a little of the bulb of cultivated fennel.

INGREDIENTS

½lb (250g) fennel stalks
salt
1 large onion, chopped
½ cup (90g) golden raisins
½ cup (90g) pine nuts
¼ tsp saffron
⅔ cup (150ml) olive oil
black pepper
6 fresh sardines
¾–1lb (375–500g) bucatini, or other long pasta
4 anchovy fillets
¼ lemon

PREPARATION

1 Wash the fennel. Put 4 quarts (4 liters) of water in a pot and add a teaspoon of salt. Bring to a boil, add the fennel stalks, and simmer for 10 minutes.
2 Put the onion in a heavy pan together with 1¾ cups (400ml) of water. Bring to a boil and simmer uncovered for 10 minutes.
3 Meanwhile, soak the raisins in warm water for 10 minutes.
4 Drain the fennel well, reserving the cooking water, and chop it fine. Add the fennel, drained raisins, pine nuts, saffron, three quarters of the oil, and plenty of pepper to the pan with the onion. Cover and cook for 15 minutes.
5 Cut off the heads and tails of the sardines and gut the fish (see page 152). Carefully remove the backbone and pick out any remaining stray bones (don't worry if the fillets fall apart).
6 Bring the water in which the fennel was cooked back to a boil and add the bucatini. Cook for 10–12 minutes, until *al dente*.
7 Meanwhile, add the sardine fillets to the sauce and cook for 5 minutes. In a separate skillet, heat the remaining oil and add the anchovies. Cook gently for 3–4 minutes, stirring continuously with a wooden spoon, until the anchovies have broken down. Add the contents of the pan to the sauce.
8 Drain the pasta, reserving 2 tablespoons of its cooking liquid. Add this to the sauce and then quickly toss the pasta in it.
9 Finish the dish with a squeeze of lemon and serve immediately.

PASTA E FAGIOLI

Pasta and beans

Technically a soup, this rustic dish is sufficiently substantial and nutritious to be a main meal in itself. It is popular throughout Italy. I have enjoyed especially fine versions in Tuscany, when fresh borlotti beans were in season, and in Naples, where all sorts of odds and ends of pasta had found their way into the dish.

INGREDIENTS

1¼ cups (250g) dried cannellini or borlotti beans, soaked overnight or two 13oz (400g) cans cooked beans, drained or 1½lb (750g) fresh beans
3 tbsp olive oil
2 celery ribs, including leaves, chopped
3oz (90g) prosciutto trimmings or pancetta, chopped
2 plump garlic cloves, chopped
2 small dried red chilies, finely chopped
1 large sprig fresh rosemary
1 tbsp tomato paste
3 tomatoes, peeled and seeded
5 cups (1.25 liters) chicken or vegetable stock (see page 155)
salt and black pepper
4oz (125g) dried pasta, such as maltagliati or spaghetti broken up into short lengths
extra-virgin olive oil and freshly grated Parmesan, to serve

PREPARATION

1 Simmer the dried beans in plenty of unsalted water for 2 hours or until soft (fresh beans take 30 minutes; canned beans need only to be rinsed).
2 Heat the oil in a heavy pan and add the celery and prosciutto. Cook over low heat for 5 minutes. Add the garlic, chilies, and rosemary and cook for 5 minutes longer.
3 Stir the tomato paste into a little warm water. Add to the pan with the tomatoes and cook for 10 minutes longer, stirring occasionally.
4 Drain the beans and add two thirds of them to the pan, together with the stock and seasoning. Bring to a boil and add the pasta. Cook uncovered for 10 minutes, until the pasta is tender.
5 Purée the remaining beans in a food processor. When the pasta is cooked, stir this purée into the soup to thicken it.
6 Serve the soup, offering small bowls of extra-virgin olive oil and Parmesan for each diner to help themselves.

VARIATIONS

• Use chickpeas instead of cannellini beans.
• Omit the rosemary and add a handful of torn basil leaves at the last minute.

ORECCHIETTE AL RAGU

Little ears with tomato sauce and meatballs

*Orecchiette, or "little ears," are the favorite pasta
of the southern Italian region of Apulia and in
particular its capital, the seaport of Bari. Served with
ragù, a slowly cooked thick tomato sauce, and meatballs,
this pasta makes an excellent winter dish.*

INGREDIENTS

3 tbsp olive oil
1 large onion, chopped
½lb (250g) slab bacon
3 garlic cloves, finely chopped
1 cup (250ml) red wine
1½lb (750g) plum tomatoes, peeled,
seeded, and chopped
13oz (400g) can whole peeled tomatoes, chopped
1 tbsp tomato paste
bouquet garni made up of 1 fresh bay leaf and 3 sprigs
each of fresh oregano, rosemary, and thyme
salt and black pepper
1lb (500g) ground beef
½ cup (60g) finely grated Parmesan, plus Parmesan to serve
½ cup (30g) fresh white bread crumbs
4 tbsp finely chopped fresh parsley
12oz–1lb (375–500g) orecchiette

PREPARATION

1 Ragù is best cooked in an earthenware pot. Heat
the oil and add the onion and the whole slab of
bacon. Cook over moderate heat for 20 minutes,
stirring frequently, until both the meat and the
onion are browned. Add two thirds of the garlic
and cook for 5 minutes longer.
2 Turn up the heat and pour in the red wine. Allow
to simmer vigorously for 5 minutes, then add both
the fresh and canned tomatoes and tomato paste.
3 Turn the heat down as low as possible, add the
bouquet garni and seasoning to taste, cover, and
cook for 2–3 hours, stirring occasionally. The
slower the sauce cooks, the better it will taste.
4 Meanwhile, mix together the ground beef,
Parmesan, bread crumbs, parsley, and remaining
garlic. Preheat the broiler. Mold the mixture into
walnut-sized balls and broil for 10 minutes, turning
them halfway through, until browned all over.
5 Add the meatballs to the tomato sauce, which
should be very thick, and cook for 30 minutes.
6 Bring 4 liters (7 pints) of salted water to a boil,
add the pasta, and cook until *al dente*.
7 Remove the bacon from the tomato sauce
(traditionally it is served as a separate main course).
Check the seasoning, pour the sauce over the
pasta, and serve with plenty of Parmesan.

Tomatoes

Red wine

Garlic

Onion

Olive
oil

Bacon

Canned
tomatoes

Tomato
paste

Bouquet garni

Salt

Black
pepper

Ground
beef

Parmesan

Bread crumbs

Parsley

Orecchiette

SPAGHETTI ALLA PUTTANESCA

Spaghetti with spicy sauce

This is known as the whores' spaghetti, though I can't imagine their business would be very good after they had eaten this garlic-laden dish. My own theory is that, because it uses items from the pantry, they were able to prepare it at the end of the night's work, before the stores opened.

INGREDIENTS

2oz (60g) anchovy fillets in olive oil
4 tbsp olive oil
4 garlic cloves, finely chopped
1 small dried chili, finely chopped
two 13oz (400g) cans whole peeled tomatoes, chopped
1 tsp dried oregano
black pepper
1 cup (125g) black olives
2 tbsp capers, rinsed and drained
¾lb–1lb (375–500g) spaghetti
salt

PREPARATION

1 Drain the anchovies and coarsely chop them. Heat the olive oil over low heat and add the anchovies. Cook, stirring constantly, until the anchovies have dissolved into the oil.
2 Turn up the heat and add the garlic and chili. As soon as the garlic begins to sizzle, add the tomatoes, oregano, and plenty of pepper. Bring the sauce to a boil, stirring continuously to help break up the tomatoes. Turn down to a gentle simmer and cook for 30 minutes, stirring continuously, until the tomatoes have broken down and made a thick sauce.
3 Meanwhile, slice the flesh from around the pits of the olives. Bring 4 quarts (4 liters) of salted water to a boil.
4 Add the spaghetti to the water and the capers and olives to the tomato sauce. When the spaghetti is *al dente*, drain it, reserving a tablespoon of the cooking water. Check the seasoning of the sauce, adding salt if necessary. Toss the pasta with the reserved cooking water and then combine it with the sauce. Serve immediately.

CANALONS

Stuffed baked pasta

It is not just the Italians who enjoy pasta – this stuffed pasta dish is a specialty of Barcelona. On Fridays the canalons are stuffed with spinach and salt cod, but the rest of the week a rich mixture of pork and chicken livers is the favorite. Illustrated on page 128.

INGREDIENTS

3 tbsp olive oil
1 onion, finely chopped
2 garlic cloves, finely chopped
8oz (250g) plum tomatoes, peeled, seeded, and chopped
¾lb (375g) finely ground pork
6oz (175g) chicken livers, finely chopped
salt and black pepper
2 pinches nutmeg
1 large egg, beaten
½ cup (30g) fresh white bread crumbs
16 canoli pasta wrappers or 12 cannelloni tubes
6 tbsp (90g) butter, plus butter to grease
½ cup (60g) all-purpose flour
2½ cups (600ml) whole milk
1 cup (90g) freshly grated Parmesan

PREPARATION

1 Heat the oil in a heavy skillet over medium heat. When the oil is hot, add the onion, reduce the heat, and cook for 25 minutes, stirring frequently, until the onion is lightly browned and caramelized.
2 Add the garlic and cook for 5 minutes, then add the tomatoes. Cook for 10 minutes longer, still stirring frequently, until the tomatoes have completely broken down. You now have the *sofregit* mixture that is the basis of so many traditional Catalan dishes.
3 Turn the heat up to medium and add the pork and chicken livers, together with the seasoning and nutmeg. Cook for 10 minutes, stirring frequently to break up the meat, until the pork and liver mixture is evenly cooked. Remove from the heat and stir in the egg and bread crumbs.
4 Bring a large pan of salted water to a boil and cook the canoli wrappers for 3 minutes or the cannelloni tubes for 4 minutes. Drain and refresh under cold water. Separate and lay on a plate.
5 Now make a roux by melting the butter and stirring in the flour. Cook over low heat for 3–4 minutes, stirring continuously, until the roux is light brown.
6 Meanwhile, warm the milk until hot. Slowly pour the milk into the roux, stirring all the time, until you have a smooth sauce. Allow to simmer for 3 minutes, still stirring continuously.

7 Preheat the oven to 350°F (180°C).

8 Grease an earthenware dish with butter. Lay a little of the meat mixture along one side of each of the canoli wrappers and roll up, placing them seam side down in the dish. Alternatively, push some filling into each of the cannelloni tubes.

9 Pour over enough white sauce to cover the canoli. Sprinkle the Parmesan over the top. Bake in the preheated oven for 45 minutes, until the surface is nicely browned and the sauce bubbling.

RISOTTO DI CARCIOFI

Artichoke risotto

In the early months of the new year, tiny purple artichokes arrive in the Venetian markets. This risotto is a favorite way of serving them, and also works well with larger globe artichokes.

INGREDIENTS

4 globe artichokes
6 tbsp (90g) butter
2 tbsp olive oil
1 small onion or 4 shallots, finely chopped
5 cups (1.25 liters) light chicken stock (see page 155)
1½ cups (300g) arborio rice
salt and black pepper
½ cup (60g) freshly grated Parmesan

PREPARATION

1 Prepare the artichokes (see page 150), then cut the hearts into very thin strips.

2 Heat 4 tbsp of butter with the oil in a large heavy pan. Gently cook the onion for 10 minutes, until soft but not browned.

3 Warm the chicken stock to simmering point in a separate pan.

4 Add the strips of artichoke and the rice to the onions or shallots, stirring well to coat the grains with the fat and adding plenty of seasoning. When the rice is thoroughly coated, pour over 1 ladleful of the simmering stock. Cook over medium heat, until all the liquid is absorbed.

5 Continue to add the hot stock, a ladleful at a time, until the rice is plump and tender but still firm to the bite. This will take 20–25 minutes – taste to check. Adjust the seasoning, then stir in the remaining butter and Parmesan, and serve.

VARIATION

• Replace the artichokes with ½lb (250g) of cleaned and thinly sliced wild mushrooms (cèpes and horns of plenty are especially good).

MEJADARRA

Rice with lentils and onions

This Lebanese dish uses simple ingredients to great effect. The key to its success is the crispy onion fried in olive oil that tops the rice and lentils. Served with chilled plain yogurt, it makes a very satisfying vegetarian main meal. Serves 4 as a main dish or 6 as a side dish.

INGREDIENTS

1 cup (250g) long-grain rice
1¼ cups (250g) brown lentils
5 large onions
⅔ cup (150ml) olive oil
1 tsp ground cumin
1 tsp ground coriander
½ tsp sweet paprika
salt and black pepper

PREPARATION

1 Soak the rice for at least an hour in plenty of water. Pick over the lentils to remove any impurities and rinse thoroughly under cold running water. Peel the onions, chop 2 of them very fine, and cut the remaining 3 in half and slice into fine half-moons.

2 Bring a large pan of water to a boil and boil the lentils for 10 minutes. Cook the finely chopped onions in 2 tbsp of oil, stirring frequently, until lightly browned all over.

3 Drain the lentils and mix in the cooked onion, spices, and plenty of seasoning. Add 6 cups (1.5 liters) of cold water, bring to a boil, and allow to boil uncovered for 10–15 minutes, until the lentils are cooked through but not disintegrating.

4 Drain and rinse the rice, and add to the pot. Boil uncovered for 5 minutes, until most of the liquid has been absorbed. Turn the heat down as low as it will go, cover, and leave for 20 minutes.

5 Meanwhile, warm the remaining oil in a skillet over medium-high heat. When it is very hot, add the onion slices and cook for 15–20 minutes, stirring frequently, until brown and caramelized.

6 Put the rice and lentil mixture in a large bowl, scatter with the crispy fried onions, and pour over the oil from the pan. Let stand for 10 minutes before serving. The dish is also good served cold.

CANALONS
Stuffed baked pasta
(page 126)

IÇ PILAVI
Pilaf with chicken livers
(page 130)

COUSCOUS AUX SEPT LEGUMES
Couscous with seven vegetables
(page 131)

IÇ PILAVI

Pilaf with chicken livers

This rich dish is of Ottoman heritage. Turkish pilafs are typically served as accompaniments to grilled meats, but this dish with chicken livers is usually served on its own. Illustrated on page 128.

INGREDIENTS

1 cup (250g) long-grain rice
6 tbsp (90g) butter
1 tbsp olive oil
1 onion, finely chopped
1 tbsp pine nuts
2 tbsp flaked almonds
½lb (250g) chicken livers, finely chopped
2 tbsp currants or raisins
1 tsp sweet paprika
salt and black pepper
2 tsp finely chopped fresh parsley

PREPARATION

1 Soak the rice in plenty of water for at least 1 hour. Drain and rinse under cold water.
2 Melt half the butter with the oil in a large heavy skillet with a lid over low heat. Add the onion and cook gently for 10 minutes, until soft.
3 Turn up the heat and add the pine nuts, almonds, and chicken livers. Cook for 5 minutes, stirring constantly, until the nuts are lightly browned and the chicken livers cooked through.
4 Melt the remaining butter in a large pan and add the rice, currants, and paprika. Cook gently for 3 minutes, stirring continuously to coat the rice grains in the oil.
5 Bring 2½ cups (600ml) of water to a boil, pour over the rice, season, stir once, and cover. Simmer gently for 12 minutes, until the water is absorbed.
6 Take the rice off the heat and stir in the chicken liver and nut mixture. Cover with a dish towel and replace the lid. Leave for 10 minutes, then fluff the rice with a fork, sprinkle with parsley, and serve.

ROZ BI SAFFRAN

Moroccan rice with dried fruit and nuts

Illustrated on page 47.

INGREDIENTS

1½ cups (375g) long-grain rice
4 tbsp butter
¼ tsp saffron
½ tsp salt
1 cup (150g) mixed pine nuts, hazelnuts, dried apricots, and raisins

PREPARATION

1 Soak the rice in plenty of water for at least 1 hour. Drain, rinse under cold water, and spread on a baking sheet to dry for 30 minutes.
2 Melt 3 tbsps of the butter in a large heavy pan with a lid. Stir in the rice and saffron.
3 Pour over 4 cups (900ml) of water, add salt, and bring rapidly to a boil. Boil for 2 minutes, then turn the heat down and cover the pan. Cook for 20 minutes, until the liquid is absorbed.
4 Take the rice off the heat and cover with a dish towel. Let stand for 10 minutes.
5 Melt the remaining butter and toss the pine nuts and hazelnuts in it for 1 minute until lightly browned. Add the dried fruit and cook for a minute longer, until warm. Stir into the rice.

TABBOULEH

Cracked wheat and herb salad

This Lebanese salad is traditionally served with crisp lettuce leaves to scoop up the herby, lemony mixture.

INGREDIENTS

1 cup (175g) fine bulgur wheat, soaked for 20–25 minutes
8 scallions, green tops removed
3 tomatoes, peeled
1 large bunch fresh parsley, stalks removed
1 small bunch fresh mint, stalks removed
juice of 2–3 lemons
¾ cup (175ml) olive oil
salt and black pepper

PREPARATION

1 Drain the bulgur wheat and squeeze dry with your hands. Finely chop the scallions, tomatoes, and herbs, then mix with the bulgur wheat.
2 Beat together the lemon juice and olive oil until emulsified, and season. Pour over the salad, adding more lemon juice if desired. Leave for 30 minutes, until the grains are tender. Serve with crisp lettuce.

COUSCOUS AUX SEPT LEGUMES

Couscous with seven vegetables·

The key to couscous is not the fine semolina grain itself, but the luxuriant sauce with which it is served. This version, from the magical Moroccan city of Fez, brings together the produce of the vegetable market in a delicately spiced broth. You can use whatever vegetables are available, but there must always be seven for luck. Serves 6–8. Illustrated on page 129.

INGREDIENTS

1 cup (175g) dried chickpeas, soaked overnight
2 lamb bones, optional
2 chicken wings, optional
3 garlic cloves, chopped
1 cinnamon stick
½ tsp saffron
½ tsp turmeric
1 tsp black pepper
6 tbsp (90g) butter
1 bunch each fresh cilantro and parsley
2 onions, grated
1lb (500g) plum tomatoes, peeled and chopped
1lb (500g) carrots, peeled
1lb (500g) small turnips, peeled
1½ cups (250g) raisins
1 tsp salt
1lb (500g) pumpkin
1lb (500g) small zucchini
4oz (125g) shelled fava beans or 4oz (125g)
shelled fresh peas
2½ cups (500g) quick-cooking couscous
harissa, to serve (see page 30)

PREPARATION

1 Place the chickpeas in a large pan or couscousière with the lamb bones and chicken wings (if using), garlic, spices, half the butter, three quarters of the herbs tied in a bunch, the onion, and tomatoes. Pour over 3½ quarts (3.5 liters) of water.
2 Bring to a boil, then reduce the heat, cover, and simmer for 1½ hours, until the chickpeas are tender.
3 Cut the carrots across at 1in (2.5cm) intervals. Halve or quarter larger turnips, leaving the very small ones whole. Remove any bones, chicken wings, and herbs from the stock and discard. Add the carrots, turnips, raisins, and the salt and continue to simmer.
4 Peel the pumpkin and cut into 2in (5cm) chunks. Cut the zucchini in half lengthwise and then in half across. Twenty minutes after adding the first group of vegetables, add the remaining ones. Simmer for 20 minutes longer.

5 Meanwhile, steam the couscous according to the package instructions (if you are using a couscousière, do this over the broth). Pile the hot couscous onto a serving dish and dot with the remaining butter.
6 Check the seasoning of the broth, adding more salt if necessary, and stir in the remaining herbs, finely chopped.
7 Serve the broth in a large tureen and allow diners to help themselves. There should also be a small pot of harissa paste on the table.

COUSCOUS AL SAMAK

Fish couscous

The Moroccans are not the only eaters of couscous – this is the classic Tunisian version. You will also find fish couscous on the western edge of Sicily, particularly in Trapani. It is a legacy of the island's Arab occupation more than a thousand years ago. Serves 6–8.

INGREDIENTS

¾ cup (125g) chickpeas
3lb (1.5 kg) mixed fish, such as red mullet,
gray mullet, sea bream, sea bass, cleaned
3 large carrots, thickly sliced
3 onions, quartered
3 small turnips, peeled and quartered
4 large plum tomatoes, quartered
¼ tsp saffron
¼–½ tsp cayenne
salt and black pepper
2½ cups (500g) quick-cooking couscous
butter, to serve

PREPARATION

1 Place the chickpeas in a pan or couscousière with 2 quarts (2 liters) of water. Bring to a boil, then simmer for 30 minutes.
2 Meanwhile, remove the heads and tails of the fish. Add these trimmings to the pot and cook for 30 minutes longer.
3 Remove the fish heads and tails from the pot and add the vegetables, saffron, cayenne, and plenty of seasoning. Simmer uncovered for 1 hour, until the vegetables are very tender.
4 Cut the fish into thick slices and add to the broth. Simmer for 10–15 minutes, until cooked through.
5 Steam the couscous according to the package instructions (if you are using a couscousière, do this over the broth). Pile the hot couscous onto a large serving dish and dot with butter. Serve with the hot fish broth.

PRESERVES

Today most foodstuffs are continuously available, but the tradition of preserving, bottling, and pickling remains and many of the products of these ancient culinary arts have become delicacies in their own right. Preserved artichoke hearts and sweet red peppers, for example, make simple but stunning antipasti; fruits bottled in sweet mustard oil, *mostardi di frutti*, are a celebrated Italian specialty; and bottled or crystallized fruits make delectable, fragrant confections popular throughout the region.

CANDIED PUMPKIN

Crystallized pumpkin is very popular in the eastern Mediterranean, especially Turkey. It can be used in baking, but is also a delicious candy. Use small pumpkins.

INGREDIENTS

2lb (1kg) slice of pumpkin
1 cup (250g) white sugar

PREPARATION

1 Remove the rind and seeds of the pumpkin. Cut the flesh into ½in (1cm) thick finger-length strips.
2 Place the sugar in a large wide pan with ⅔ cup (150ml) of water. Bring slowly to a boil, stirring continuously so that the sugar dissolves.
3 Arrange the pumpkin strips in a single layer. Simmer gently in the syrup for 45 minutes, stirring frequently to prevent the strips of pumpkin from sticking together. The pumpkin should be very soft and translucent.
4 Arrange the strips of pumpkin on waxed paper on a baking sheet, making sure the strips are not touching. Preheat the oven to 200°F (95°C). Leave the pumpkin slices in the oven overnight, or for 10–12 hours. Remove from the oven and allow to cool – the pumpkin will become crisp. It will keep in an airtight container for up to 3 months.

VARIATION

• Instead of drying the slices of pumpkin in the oven, allow them to cool in the syrup, to which you have added 2 tsp of rose water. Serve in very small quantities with whipped cream and walnuts.

CONSERVA DI PEPERONI

Preserved peppers

Although peppers are now available all year, they are still worth preserving. Peppers kept in this way develop a concentrated sweetness, making them ideal as a little antipasto, served with a few marinated olives and a slice of good bread.

INGREDIENTS

2lb (1kg) red peppers
2 tbsp coarse sea salt
handful of fresh basil leaves

PREPARATION

1 Broil the peppers until the skins are blackened and then peel them (see page 150).
2 Rinse the peeled peppers thoroughly under cold water. Cut the flesh into strips.
3 Pack the peppers into a sterilized lidded canning jar into which they just fit, layering with the salt and basil leaves. Screw on the lid.
4 Place the jar in a pan, cover it with cold water, bring to a boil, and boil for 15 minutes. The peppers will keep for up to 6 months.

VARIATION

• The Italians preserve peppers in white wine vinegar – *peperoni sott' aceto*. Pour a bottle of good quality wine vinegar into a pan and bring to a boil. Add 4–6 cored, sliced sweet red peppers and simmer for 15 minutes. Season with salt and pour into a sterilized canning jar. Tuck in a few fresh bay leaves and leave for 2 months before using.

DULCE DE MEMBRILLO

Quince paste

This thick orange-colored paste, heavy with the perfume of quinces, is often served in Spain with a slice of Manchego cheese as a snack or to end a meal.

INGREDIENTS

4lb (2kg) quinces
white sugar
butter, to grease baking sheet

PREPARATION

1 Peel and core the quinces. Roughly chop the flesh and put it in a heavy pan with ½ cup (125ml) of water. Bring the water to a boil, turn down to a simmer, cover, and cook for 30 minutes.
2 At the end of this time you will have a purée. Push it through a sieve to remove lumps.
3 Measure the purée and stir in 1 cup (275g) of sugar per 2 cups (500g) of pulp. Return to the pan and simmer for 45 minutes, uncovered.
4 Pour the mixture into a lightly greased oblong baking sheet, to the depth of about 1in (2.5cm). Let cool and cut into squares. It will keep for up to 1 month stored in a jar or wrapped in waxed paper.

MARINATED OLIVES

Store-bought olives in brine can sometimes seem a little dull. To improve their flavor, bottle them in oil infused with fragrant herbs and garlic, or perhaps add some small dried red chilies and orange zest.

INGREDIENTS

4 cups (500g) mixed black and green olives
2 garlic cloves, peeled
1 sprig fresh thyme
1 sprig fresh rosemary
1 fresh bay leaf
1 piece lemon zest
1¾ cups (450ml) extra-virgin olive oil, to cover

PREPARATION

1 Rinse the olives well, then pack them in a canning jar together with the garlic, herbs, and lemon zest. Pour in sufficient olive oil to cover.
2 Leave for 2–3 weeks for the flavors to develop. Olives keep for up to 6 months.

PRESERVED LEMONS

The sharpness of lemon juice plays a key part in Mediterranean cookery. It is difficult to imagine this region without its groves of citrus fruit trees, but the lemon and orange were first introduced to the area by the Romans who brought seedlings from India. The Moors revitalized their popularity, planting groves in Sicily and southern Spain. Today the Moroccans preserve lemons in salt for use in fragrant tagines.

INGREDIENTS

6 lemons
½ cup (125g) coarse sea salt
1 fresh bay leaf
2 cloves
6 coriander seeds
6 black peppercorns
freshly squeezed lemon juice, to cover

PREPARATION

1 Soak the lemons in water for 2 days, changing the water once.
2 Quarter the lemons from the top to within ½in (1cm) of the bottom. Sprinkle plenty of salt onto the cut flesh, then reassemble the lemons.
3 Place half the remaining salt in a sterilized canning jar, then pack in the lemons, bay leaf, and spices. Add the remaining salt and press down on the lemons to release their juices.
4 Top with just enough lemon juice to cover and leave for at least 1 month and up to 6 months.
5 Rinse well before use to remove excess salt.

Conserva di Peperoni

Preserved Lemons

DESSERTS

Sweet dishes are typically eaten separately in the Mediterranean, rather than at the end of the meal. Sticky pastries, laden with honey, are usually enjoyed with a cup of coffee in a bakery; ice cream is eaten at the *gelateria* or the *heladeria*. The meal itself often ends with a simple bowl of fruit, or a dessert made from those fruits. What could be nicer and more refreshing than wild strawberries served in a chilled glass of red wine, figs baked with scented honey, or peaches stuffed with almond paste?

SIKA STO FOURNO

Baked figs

A fresh fig is one of the greatest treats that the Mediterranean region has to offer — especially if it is eaten almost as soon as it is picked from the tree on which it has ripened to perfection. In Greece, slightly underripe figs are baked with a little scented honey from the sacred mount of Hymettus to bring out their full flavor.

INGREDIENTS

8 figs
juice of 1 orange
½ cup (125ml) Samos or other sweet wine
2 tbsp clear honey, preferably Hymettus honey
2 tbsp orange-flower water, optional
Greek plain yogurt or sour cream, to serve

PREPARATION

1 Preheat the oven to 300°F (150°C).
2 Make deep crosses in the top of the figs and place them in a gratin dish in which they just fit.
3 Gently heat together the orange juice, wine, and honey and pour this over the figs, making sure plenty gets down into the cracks.
4 Bake the figs in the oven for 40 minutes, spooning over the juices several times, until the figs are very soft. Sprinkle over the orange-flower water, if desired, and serve with creamy yogurt.

VARIATION

• Serve the figs with fresh heavy cream slightly sweetened with superfine sugar and infused with a few strands of saffron soaked in a little warm water.

PERAS ESTOFADOS

Poached pears

This is a beautiful dish — the poached pears burnished gold with honey and dark Oloroso sherry sit in a pool of syrup redolent with cinnamon and saffron.

INGREDIENTS

8 slightly underripe pears
juice and grated zest of 1 lemon
1 cup (250g) honey
¾ cup (175ml) Oloroso sherry
2 cloves
1 cinnamon stick
pinch of saffron
8 blanched almonds, optional

PREPARATION

1 Peel the pears and pack them upright in a heavy pan. Pour over the lemon juice.
2 Mix together the remaining ingredients with 2½ cups (600ml) of water and boil for 5–10 minutes, until a syrup forms. Pour this mixture over the pears, bring back to a boil, and then turn down to a bare simmer. Poach the pears gently for 20 minutes, leaving the pan uncovered.
3 Discard the cinnamon stick and cloves. Remove the pears and reduce the syrup by fast boiling for 5 minutes. Return the pears to the liquid and let cool. Before serving, replace the stems of the pears with the blanched almonds, if desired.

PESCHE RIPIENE

Stuffed peaches

A perfect peach should be enjoyed just as it is. But even in Italy not all peaches are perfect, so underripe ones are stuffed with a macaroon mixture and baked in white wine.

INGREDIENTS

4 peaches
2 almond macaroons
8 blanched almonds
1 egg yolk
3 tbsp superfine sugar
1 tsp grated lemon zest
butter, to coat dish
½ cup (100ml) sweet white wine
flaked almonds, optional

PREPARATION

1 Halve the peaches and remove the pit. Scoop out a little of the flesh to make a deeper hole.
2 Put the macaroons, almonds, egg yolk, two tablespoons of sugar, the lemon zest, and the scooped-out peach flesh in a food processor and work until you have a smooth paste. Stuff the hollows in the peaches with this mixture.
3 Preheat the oven to 325°F (160°C). Lightly butter an earthenware ovenproof dish and arrange the stuffed peaches in it. Pour over the wine and sprinkle the peaches with the remaining sugar. Bake for 30 minutes.
4 Meanwhile, toast the flaked almonds under a hot broiler. Remove the peaches from the oven and let them cool in the liquid. Serve warm or at room temperature, sprinkled with almonds.

FRAISES DE BOIS AU VIN ROUGE

Provençal wild strawberries in red wine

In the western Mediterranean, dessert is often fruit marinated in wine or spirits – perhaps peaches or nectarines in Sauternes, blueberries with grappa, or this favorite of mine, tiny wild strawberries in chilled red wine.

INGREDIENTS

1lb (500g) wild or small strawberries, rinsed and dried
2 tbsp superfine sugar
2 glasses Beaujolais or other light, fruity red wine
4 fresh mint leaves

PREPARATION

1 Sprinkle the strawberries with sugar and place them in 4 tall wine glasses.
2 Pour in sufficient Beaujolais to cover the berries. Decorate with a mint leaf and chill thoroughly.

KHOSHAF

Dried fruit and nut salad

This Lebanese specialty is made distinctive by the perfumed marinade that infuses the dried fruit.

INGREDIENTS

2 cups (375g) dried apricots
1 cup (175g) seedless raisins
½ cup (125g) superfine sugar
1 tbsp rose water
1 tbsp orange-flower water
1 cup (175g) blanched almonds or a mixture of almonds and pistachio nuts

PREPARATION

1 Place the dried fruits in a large bowl and sprinkle over the sugar and the scented waters.
2 Pour in just enough cold water to cover the fruits and leave in a warm place for 48 hours.
3 Add the nuts and chill well before serving.

SALADE D'ORANGES

Orange salad

INGREDIENTS

6 navel oranges
2 tbsp orange-flower water
2 tbsp confectioner's sugar
2 tsp ground cinnamon

TARTE AU CITRON

Lemon tart

Though lemon tart is now popular throughout France, especially in the brasseries of Paris, it is only in the south that the lemon trees grow. Wherever it is made, it truly captures the sparkling flavor of the lemon.

INGREDIENTS

2 cups (250g) all-purpose flour
pinch of salt
1 cup (200g) superfine sugar
½ cup (125g) unsalted butter
1 egg yolk, plus 5 eggs, separated
¼ cup (60ml) ice water
zest and juice of 3 lemons
1 tsp cornstarch

PREPARATION

1 Sift the flour with the salt and ⅓ cup (90g) of sugar. Cut the butter into small cubes and crumble it into the flour with your fingers.
2 Make a well in the center of the butter and flour mixture and add the egg yolk and the ice water. Stir well until you have a smooth paste. Wrap in plastic wrap and chill for 1 hour.
3 Beat the remaining egg yolks with ⅓ cup (90g) of sugar until light and creamy. Add the zest and juice of the lemons and then carefully stir in the cornstarch, ensuring there are no lumps. Pour into a heavy-based pan and heat gently for 5 minutes, stirring constantly, until the mixture thickens – do not allow the mixture to boil or it will curdle.
4 Preheat the oven to 350°F (180°C). Roll out the pastry until thin and line a buttered 10in (25cm) tart pan. Prick the base of the pastry all over with a fork, weigh it down with dried beans, and bake for 15 minutes.
5 Beat the egg whites with the remaining sugar until stiff. Gently fold the egg whites into the lemon cream, then pour this mixture into the pastry shell. Bake for 20–25 minutes, until the surface is lightly browned all over. Serve warm or cold.

PREPARATION

1 Peel the oranges and remove any pith. Slice them across very fine and arrange on a plate in overlapping circles.
2 Sprinkle over the orange-flower water, confectioner's sugar, and half the cinnamon. Chill the salad for at least 2 hours.
3 Just before serving, sprinkle the remaining cinnamon over the oranges.

FLAN DE NARANJA

Baked orange custard

The first orange groves planted in Spain yielded bitter oranges, which came to be known after the town of Seville. This delicate orange custard owes its special flavor to the inclusion of juice from a Seville orange as well as that from the more familiar sweet oranges.

INGREDIENTS

¾ cup (150g) sugar
5 eggs
juice of 3 sweet oranges and 1 Seville orange,
approximately 2 cups (450ml)
2 tsp orange-flower water, optional
1 tsp grated orange zest

PREPARATION

1 Mix ⅓ cup (90g) of sugar with 2 tsp of water in a saucepan. Warm over medium heat, shaking the pan from time to time, until the sugar has turned a light golden color. Do not let it burn.
2 Pour the caramelized sugar into an 8in (20cm) oval flan dish or a 7in (18cm) round dish (you could also use 4 individual dishes).
3 To make the custard, whisk the eggs with the remaining sugar until light and creamy. Carefully stir in the orange juice, orange-flower water, if using, and zest.
4 Preheat the oven to 300°F (150°C). Pour the custard into the flan dish, and then place this in a roasting pan filled with enough warm water to come halfway up the side of the dish.
5 Bake the custard in the oven for 1 hour, until it is set and a skewer inserted into it comes out clean. Let cool completely before turning it out onto a serving dish. The custard should be topped with a layer of runny caramel.

RAHAT LOKUM

Turkish delight

This sweet, sticky treat was for centuries the delight of the women of the harems. Serve with cardamom coffee.

INGREDIENTS

2¼ cups (500g) sugar
juice of ½ lemon
4 envelopes unflavored gelatin: approximately 1oz (30g)
2 tbsp rose water
butter, to coat baking sheet
¾ cup (60g) blanched pistachio nuts, chopped
½ cup (60g) confectioner's sugar
2 tbsp cornstarch

PREPARATION

1 Mix the sugar and 1¼ cups (300ml) of water in a saucepan. Add the lemon juice. Heat slowly to dissolve the sugar, then bring to a boil.
2 Continue to boil, without stirring, until the temperature reaches 250–265°F (120–130°C) on a candy thermometer, or until a little dropped into cold water forms a hard ball. Remove from the heat. Do not allow the mixture to caramelize.
3 Place the pan in a bowl of ice water and let cool for 10 minutes.
4 Dissolve the gelatin in ½ cup (125ml) of hot water and then stir the gelatin solution and rose water into the syrup.
5 Lightly butter a 6in (15cm) square baking pan. Pour in half the syrup, then sprinkle with nuts. Cover with the remaining syrup and let cool. When cool, place in the refrigerator for 24 hours.
6 Cut the set mixture into squares. Sift together the confectioner's sugar and cornstarch and roll the squares in it. Let dry on a baking sheet for 24 hours. Store in an airtight container.

SEPHARDI TAMAR

Stuffed dates

Fresh dates are made even more luxurious in Israel, where they are pitted and stuffed with a nugget of almond-flavored paste. This little confection is perfect with a cup of coffee.

INGREDIENTS

16 fresh dates
3 tbsp ground almonds
1 tbsp finely chopped pistachio nuts
1 tbsp superfine sugar
2 tbsp unsalted butter, softened

PREPARATION

1 With a sharp knife, make a slit down the center of each date and carefully remove the pit.
2 Mix together the almonds, pistachio nuts, sugar, and butter, adding a very little water so that you have a smooth paste.
3 Fashion the paste into nuggets the size of date pits and use these to stuff the dates. Chill thoroughly before serving.

VARIATION

• Pour a syrup of ½ cup (125g) sugar, 2 tbsp clear honey, 2 tbsp lemon juice, and ¾ cup (175ml) of water over the dates, then chill.

BAKLAVA

Pastry with nuts

The original baklava was made up of 40 sheets of pastry, symbolizing the 40 days of Lent, and was traditionally eaten on Easter Day. Its popularity spread and baklava soon became a favorite with Turkish sultans, who relished the buttery pastry in its sweet sticky syrup.

INGREDIENTS

1 cup (200g) sugar
4 tbsp clear honey
juice of ½ lemon
2 tbsp rose water
½lb (250g) unsalted butter
1 tsp cinnamon
2 cups (375g) shelled, blanched walnuts, pistachios, or almonds, roughly chopped
12oz (375g) package phyllo pastry

PREPARATION

1 Put the sugar, honey, lemon juice, and 2 cups (450ml) of water in a pan and bring to a boil.

Boil uncovered for 8–10 minutes, until the syrup is thick enough to coat the back of a spoon. Stir in the rose water and let cool.

2 Melt the butter and skim off the foam that rises to the surface. Mix the cinnamon into the nuts. Preheat the oven to 350°F (180°C).

3 Lay a sheet of pastry in a 12 x 7in (30 x 18cm) baking sheet and brush with melted butter. Repeat with another 3 sheets, then sprinkle over a third of the nuts. Cover with 4 more sheets of pastry, brushing each time with butter, then add the second third of the nuts. Repeat the process with the remaining nuts and pastry, brushing the last piece liberally with butter.

4 With a knife, make deep diagonal crosses across the top of the baklava to make diamond shapes.

5 Bake the baklava for 30 minutes, then lower the oven temperature to 300°F (150°C). Bake for 45 minutes longer, until the top of the phyllo pastry is nicely browned.

6 Pour over the cool syrup, making sure plenty gets down between the cracks. Let the baklava cool before serving.

GRANITA DI COCOMERO

Watermelon granita

The Sicilians are credited with bringing water ices to Italy, having learned the art of making it from their Arab invaders. The granita is closest to those original ices, being a frozen sherbet. This pale pink watermelon granita is a particular favorite in Sicily.

INGREDIENTS

2lb (1kg) slice of watermelon
1 cup (250g) superfine sugar
juice of ½ lemon
1 tbsp orange-flower water
½ tsp ground cinnamon, optional

PREPARATION

1 Remove the seeds and rind of the watermelon. Purée the flesh in a food processor.
2 Mix together the sugar and ⅔ cup (150ml) of water and bring to a boil. Simmer for 5 minutes, then take off the heat and stir in the lemon juice, orange-flower water, and cinnamon. Let cool.
3 Combine the cooled syrup with the watermelon purée. Pour into a mold and place in the freezer.
4 Stir the mixture every 15 minutes for 2 hours, then every 30 minutes for another hour, or until the granita has nearly frozen solid but still has a slightly slushy consistency. Serve, or if you wish to leave the granita in the freezer longer, remove it an hour before serving so that it is not set solid.

MENU PLANNING

Mediterranean cooks do not tend to stick to rigid menus – what is chosen for a meal will in large part have been dictated by what was good in the market that day. This approach does require flexibility, but is invariably successful. The twelve menus here are intended to be starting points, and include both ideas for regional themes and suggestions for specific social occasions.

PROVENCE

As you cook, the aromas of herbs and wine will evoke images of Provence in summer. This is a menu for the savvy shopper, using fresh produce cooked simply to allow flavor to shine through.

Soupe au Pistou (page 64)
Vegetable soup with pistou sauce *or*

Beignets de Fleurs de Courgette (page 84)
Zucchini flower fritters with fresh tomato sauce

•

Loup de Mer Grillé au Fenouil (page 93)
Sea bass grilled with fennel *or*

Poulet Sauté aux Herbes de Provence (page 111)
Chicken sautéed with herbs and
garlic in white wine

Mesclun (page 77)
Salad of young leaves

•

Fraises de Bois au Vin Rouge (page 136)
Wild strawberries in red wine

SPAIN

This menu offers at the first and main course stage a choice of dishes from the Catalan and Andalusian coasts of Spain, two regions that guard their different culinary traditions jealously.

Escalivada (page 88)
Catalan roasted peppers, eggplant, and onions *or*

Gazpacho Andaluz (page 36)
Andalusian gazpacho

•

Romesco de Peix (page 98)
Seafood stew with romesco pepper sauce *or*

Pato a la Sevillana (page 115)
Duck with olives, orange, and sherry

•

Dulce de Membrillo (page 133) with Manchego cheese
Quince paste

•

Peras Estofados (page 134)
Poached pears

Poulet Sauté aux Herbes de Provence

Gazpacho Andaluz

ITALY

A traditional meal in Italy starts with antipasti, moves on to pasta, soup, or a risotto, and proceeds to the main course, often a simple grilled meat or fish dish. Fruit or ice cream follows – then a siesta.

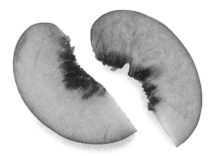

Bruschetta (page 120) with mixed salamis, pickled vegetables, and olives
Garlic bread with antipasti

———•———

Gnocchi al Pesto (page 42)
Italian potato dumplings with pesto sauce **or**

Risotto di Carciofi (page 127)
Artichoke risotto

———•———

Zuppa di Pesce (page 34)
Italian fish soup **or**

La Pizzaiola (page 108)
Steak with tomato sauce

———•———

Pesche Ripiene (page 135)
Stuffed peaches

Zuppa di Pesce

NORTH AFRICA

North African food is ideal for large gatherings – a fragrant tagine and a couscous to which everyone helps themselves make for a convivial evening. Most of the menu can be made in advance.

Salata Jazar (page 74) with flat bread
Carrot salad

•

Tagine d'Agneau aux Abricots (page 118)
Tagine of lamb with apricots **or**

Djej Emshmel (page 46)
Tagine of chicken with lemons and olives

•

Couscous aux Sept Légumes (page 131)
Couscous with seven vegetables

•

Salade d'Oranges (page 136)
Orange salad

Djej Emshmel

GREECE AND TURKEY

These two countries may be separated only by the narrow Aegean Sea, but Greece has always looked west for its culinary inspiration, while Turkey looks to the east. Their cuisines have much in common, but each remains distinctive.

Anginares me Koukia (page 76) with flat bread
Greek salad of artichokes with baby fava beans *or*

Yoğurtlu Patlican (page 88)
Turkish fried eggplant with yogurt

———•———

Moussaka (page 114)
Baked eggplant layered with lamb *or*

Iç Pilavi (page 130)
Pilaf with chicken livers

———•———

Sika sto Fourno (page 134)
Baked figs *or*

Baklava (page 138) and Rahat Lokum (page 137)
Pastry with nuts and Turkish delight

———•———

Turkish coffee

EASTERN MEDITERRANEAN

Meals in the east of the region usually start with a selection of little dishes eaten with bread. These *meze* are followed by meat or fish, often served with rice. Fresh fruit or marinated dried fruit are popular desserts.

Salata il Shamonder (page 74)
Beet salad

Baba Ghanouj (page 70)
Lebanese eggplant and sesame dip

Hummus bi Tahini (page 70)
Chickpea and sesame dip

Tabbouleh (page 130) with lettuce and flat bread
Lebanese cracked wheat and herb salad

———•———

Daoud Pasha (page 110)
Syrian spicy lamb meatballs with pine nuts in tomato sauce *or*

Samak Meshwi bi Tahini (page 92) with rice
Grilled fish with sesame sauce

———•———

Khoshaf (page 136)
Dried fruit and nut salad

Baba Ghanouj

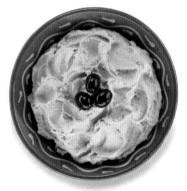

Baklava **Hummus bi Tahini**

SUMMER LUNCH

On a hot summer's day, Mediterranean food comes into its own. You can prepare first courses and desserts in advance and then leave some fish to bake in the oven or over the grill while you sit back and enjoy the sun.

Çaçik Soupa (page 60)
Cold soup of yogurt and cucumber *or*

Ratatouille (page 81) served cold
Vegetables stewed in olive oil

•

Rougets à la Niçoise (page 56)
Red mullet Niçois style *or*

Samak Charmoula (page 103)
Marinated and baked fish

•

Granita di Cocomero (page 139)
Watermelon granita

Rougets à la Niçoise

PICNIC

Combine a few easily transportable cooked dishes with some good country bread, a little cheese or salami, and some luscious fresh fruit to refresh the palate, and you have everything you need for a leisurely summer picnic.

Pan Bagnat (page 68)
Salade niçoise in a roll

•

Tortilla (page 85)
Spanish potato omelet

•

Pissaladière (page 48)
Provençal onion tart *or*

Spanakopita (page 89)
Spinach pie

•

Selection of goat cheeses and salamis, with marinated olives and country bread

•

Fresh figs and grapes

Pan Bagnat

BARBECUE

Fish or meat marinated in olive oil and garlic and grilled over charcoal makes a healthful and delicious meal on a hot day. The only accompaniments you need are bread, a crisp salad, fruit, and perhaps a cooling ice to finish.

Sardalya Sarmasi (page 102)
Stuffed sardines in grape leaves *or*

Kiliç siste Tarator (page 92)
Swordfish kebabs with walnut sauce

———•———

Şiş Köftesi (page 106)
Ground meat on skewers *or*

Djej Meshwi (page 106)
Grilled spring chicken

———•———

Country or flat bread

———•———

Salata Horiatiki (page 75)
Peasant salad

———•———

Fruit or Granita di Cocomero (page 139)
Watermelon granita

Salata Horiatiki

SUPPER FOR FRIENDS

To my mind, a simple supper with friends or family sitting around the kitchen table is the best way to eat Mediterranean food. This is food prepared with the minimum of fuss to give the maximum amount of pleasure.

Soupe de Potiron (page 61)
Pumpkin soup *or*

Bruschetta (page 120)
Garlic bread

———•———

Chakchouka (page 81) with bread
Spicy peppers and tomatoes with eggs *or*

Parmigiana (page 87)
Eggplant baked with mozzarella
and Parmesan

———•———

Flan de Naranja (page 137)
Baked orange custard *or*

Sika sto Fourno (page 134)
Baked figs

Parmigiana

CELEBRATORY DINNER PARTY

This is a menu for a special occasion, using high quality ingredients to produce a luxurious meal. It does require some last-minute cooking, but none of the dishes takes long to prepare.

Huevos Revueltos con Esparragos (page 88)
Scrambled eggs with asparagus

———— • ————

Coquilles St. Jacques à la Provençale (page 97)
Scallops with garlic and Cognac

———— • ————

Soumanate bi'Leinab (page 109) with rice
Quail with grapes

———— • ————

Ensalada Sevillana (page 76)
Sevillian salad

———— • ————

Selection of goat cheeses

———— • ————

Tarte au Citron (page 136)
Lemon tart

Soumanate bi' Leinab

COCKTAIL PARTY

The nibbles served as *antipasti, meze,* or *tapas* around the Mediterranean are ideal for parties, when the need is for tasty finger food. This menu gives a good balance of hot and cold foods.

Marinated olives (page 133)

———— • ————

Crostini di Fegato (page 71)
Tuscan chicken liver toasts

———— • ————

Crostini with Tapenade (page 66)
and Anchoïade (page 67)
Toasts with olive and caper paste
and anchovy paste

———— • ————

Tortilla (page 85), cut into squares
Spanish potato omelet

———— • ————

Böreks (page 72)
Turkish pastries

———— • ————

Pinchos Morunos (page 107)
Pork kebabs

———— • ————

Albondigas (page 110)
Pork and parsley meatballs

———— • ————

Dolmathes (page 72)
Stuffed grape leaves

Tortilla

TECHNIQUES

*Mediterranean food rarely requires complicated
cooking techniques. Much of the cook's work is in the
preparation of ingredients, perhaps trimming artichokes,
preparing squid, or splitting chickens for the grill. This
section demonstrates how quick and simple these
tasks can be. An illustrated "photo album" of equipment
also features some of the traditional utensils found in
Mediterranean kitchens and offers advice on choosing
some of the more basic and indispensable items.*

COOKING EQUIPMENT

A typical Mediterranean kitchen does not contain a great deal of specialist cooking equipment, but some basic items do make life appreciably easier, and may even help improve the flavor of the food you are preparing. A few slightly more unusual pieces of equipment are also useful for specific dishes.

> ### OTHER USEFUL EQUIPMENT
> *cutting board, marble or wooden; grinders for pepper and coarse salt; coffee grinder, for coffee beans and whole spices; wooden and slotted spoons; colander and sieves*

Flat-blade skewers

SKEWERS
Flat-blade and round metal skewers are excellent for broiling and grilling meat or fish – the metal conducts the heat, ensuring that the food is cooked through. Wooden skewers can be used for small kebabs and for splitting small birds (see page 155).

POTS AND PANS
As a general rule, thick-based kitchenware suits the country-style cooking of much Mediterranean food. Unglazed earthenware pots give food a distinctive flavor – keep a round earthenware pot with handles to use over direct heat and several smaller round or oval dishes for baking. Enameled casseroles are also useful. A large heavy cast-iron frying pan with a long handle is extremely versatile.

KNIVES
Use a small short-blade knife for vegetables and a larger knife with a long thick blade for meat, a small blunt knife for scaling fish and a mezzaluna, a crescent-shaped, double-handled rocking knife for chopping herbs.

Heavy cast-iron frying pan

Paellera

Mezzaluna

PAELLERA
The paellera is a shallow two-handled pan, traditionally made of iron. It is distinguished by its size – usually paellas are made in lavish sizes. Like all cast-iron utensils, it should be kept oiled when not in use.

COUSCOUSIERE
This steamer allows you to cook the grains of couscous over the spicy stew with which they will be served.

EARTHENWARE CASSEROLE
An earthenware pot with a lid is excellent for oven cooking as it retains heat, flavor, and moisture.

TAGINE
Used for the Moroccan stews to which it has lent its name, the tagine is an earthenware dish with a conical lid and a large round base.

MORTAR AND PESTLE
A large marble mortar and pestle is invaluable for pastes. Wooden and stone mortars are also useful. Choose a small mortar with a ridged base for crushing spices.

TIAN
The tian is a shallow oval earthenware dish, used for the Provençal gratins to which it has lent its name (see page 103).

Grill pan's ridges sear the food

GRILL PAN
A cast-iron grill pan is used for cooking Spanish-style on the hot plate.

PREPARING VEGETABLES

Certain vegetables need extra attention. Delicate lettuce leaves, for example, should be washed, then dried by shaking in a dish towel; mushrooms should be wiped with a damp cloth – never immerse them in water.

PEELING TOMATOES

Plunge the tomatoes into boiling water for 45 seconds, then drain. Pierce the skin at the top with a knife. Score to the bottom, then peel off the skin. To seed tomatoes, cut them in half lengthwise and scoop out the seeds.

PEELING RED PEPPERS

Preheat the broiler to high. Broil the pepper, turning it frequently, until the skin is thoroughly blackened, about 20 minutes. Remove and cover with a clean dish towel for 10 minutes. Peel off the blistered skin with your fingers.

SALTING AND BLOTTING

Certain vegetables, such as eggplant and zucchini, have bitter juices. This process draws those juices out. Slice the vegetables as instructed in the recipe. Place in a colander and sprinkle with coarse salt, about 2 tsp per eggplant, 1 tsp per zucchini. Cover with a plate and place a heavy weight on top. Let drain for 30–45 minutes. Rinse well and pat dry with paper towels.

MAKING SAUCES

Cold sauces such as pesto are best made in a mortar and pestle. Pound the first elements, often garlic and sea salt, until they break down. Add the remaining ingredients and crush to make a paste.

PREPARING ARTICHOKES

1 Bend back the tough outer leaves of the artichoke so that they snap off. (This is the only necessary preparation technique for baby artichokes.)

2 Using a sharp knife, slice horizontally through the leaves 1in (2.5cm) from the base of the artichoke.

3 Cut the stalk off at the base. Scrape out the small central leaves and hairy "choke" and discard. Rinse, then place in water with lemon juice added.

DOUGH AND PASTRY

Variations of bread dough are used in many regional specialties, from Pissaladière (see page 48) to pizzas. The preparation techniques are broadly similar.

Pastry, too, requires a few basic skills that are applicable to a wide range of dishes. Making phyllo pastry is an art in itself; the ready-made frozen product is excellent.

KNEADING AND PUNCHING DOWN DOUGH

1 Prepare the dough according to the recipe. Flour your hands and begin to work the dough on a floured surface, pressing the dough with your knuckles and turning it over and over.

2 When the dough loses its stickiness and reaches a smooth, pliable consistency, place it in an oiled bowl, cover with a clean dish towel, and leave in a warm place to rise.

3 When the dough has doubled in size (approximately 1 hour), lightly punch it down with your knuckles to expel the air. Some recipes will require you to knead it again.

MAKING PHYLLO PASTRY BUNDLES

1 Place a strip of pastry on a dry surface. Brush with melted or clarified butter. Place some filling on the bottom right-hand corner, about ¾in (2cm) from the edge. Pick up the corner.

2 Fold the bottom right-hand corner over the filling to make a triangle. Carefully pick up the corner of the triangle in your thumb and forefinger, keeping the filling intact.

3 Continue folding the triangle across and up the strip, being careful not to lose any filling, until you reach the end of the strip.

Crisp phyllo pastry bundles

4 Brush the triangle with melted or clarified butter, then bake.

FISH AND SHELLFISH

Make a friend at the fish store and you will receive expert advice on what is best from the catch of the day and assistance in its preparation. If you do have to gut and clean fish yourself, make sure you wash them out thoroughly.

When buying shellfish, choose raw whole shrimp, fresh if available, and cook and peel them yourself. Buy crabs and lobsters alive and cook them at home to ensure freshness. Pre-cooked lobsters should be eaten on the day they were cooked.

CLEANING FISH

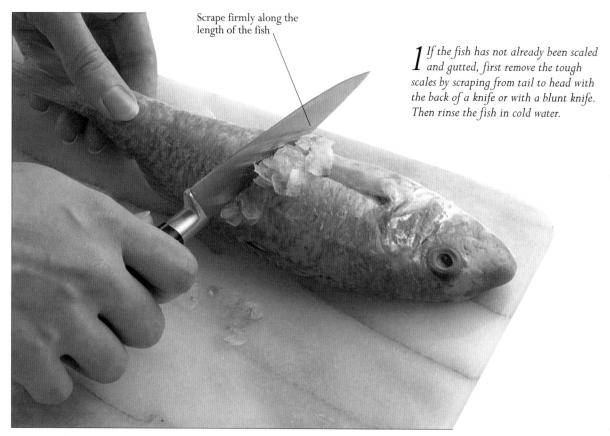

Scrape firmly along the length of the fish

1 If the fish has not already been scaled and gutted, first remove the tough scales by scraping from tail to head with the back of a knife or with a blunt knife. Then rinse the fish in cold water.

2 Using a small sharp knife, make a slit up along the length of the belly to the gills. Cut off the gills.

3 Grasp the innards between your thumb and forefinger and pull them out of the cavity.

4 Holding the fish open, rinse the cavity under cold running water to remove traces of blood.

PREPARING SQUID

 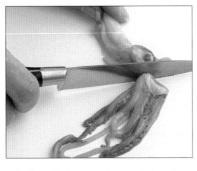 

1 Hold the base of the head and pull out the attached innards from the body sac. Discard the head and innards and rinse the body inside and out.

2 Cut off the tentacles just below the eyes, taking care to remove the hard inedible "beak," and set aside.

3 Peel off the mottled outer skin, together with the "wings," to reveal the milky white flesh.

4 Pull out the transparent plasticlike "bone" that runs vertically along the body sac. Rinse well again. Cut up the tentacles and white flesh as described in the recipe.

CLEANING MUSSELS AND CLAMS

1 Place mussels and clams in salted water to allow them to disgorge grit. Discard any that fail to open or are broken.

2 Scrub the shellfish with a small stiff brush to remove any barnacles or dirt attached to the outer shell.

3 For mussels, pull out the small strands that protrude from one side of the shell. This is known as "debearding."

CLEANING SCALLOPS

1 Scallops are tricky to open and prepare. If you do buy uncleaned scallops, pry apart the shell halves with a small blunt knife. Be careful not to damage the flesh.

2 With a sharp knife, cut the white muscle away from the shell, then cut away the inedible membranes. Keep the edible coral intact. Rinse all traces of grit away under cold running water.

The scallop is now ready to·be cooked on the shell under a broiler, or cooked separately and then returned to its shell.

MEAT

The way that animals are raised, fed, slaughtered, aged, and finally prepared for the table affects the taste of the meat — look for a good butcher to help you find the best products. Corn-fed chickens, for example, have a superior flavor, and game that has been aged is far more tender. If you are barbecuing meat, leave on a little fat as it provides flavor and keeps in moisture during cooking. When cooking a roast, allow it to rest for 10–15 minutes before carving and serving it.

CUTTING UP CHICKEN

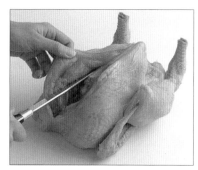

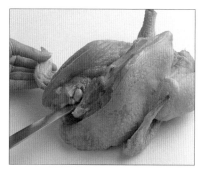

1 Make an incision down the breast-bone toward the tail end. Cut down the side of the breastbone to loosen the flesh. Remove the wishbone.

2 Cut down until you reach the wing joint, then slice through it. Put the tip of your knife in the wing socket and push away the breast.

3 Begin to separate the whole side from the frame of the carcass by cutting downward through the skin and flesh then pulling away the side.

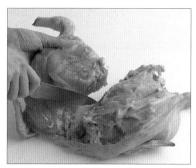

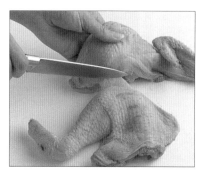

4 Cut down through the leg joint and break it away from the main carcass, then cut away the whole side.

5 Cut around the thigh and leg joint, separating it from the breast and wing. Remove the wing tips and discard.

6 Cut away the wing, leaving a little breast attached. Make a cut between the thigh and drumstick, then divide.

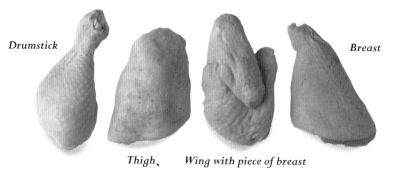

Drumstick

Breast

Thigh,   *Wing with piece of breast*

Chicken cut into 8 pieces

7 Repeat with the other side. You now have 8 pieces of chicken. To make 16 easy-to-eat pieces, chop both the legs and thighs in half, chop both breast pieces in half again, and add any choice scraps.

SPLITTING SMALL BIRDS FOR GRILLING

1 Place the bird on a cutting board breast side down. With a sharp knife, split the bird by cutting all the way along the backbone.

2 Turn the bird over and flatten it out by pressing down on the breastbone with the heel of your hand in order to crack it.

3 Secure the bird flat by pushing a skewer through it from the wing tip on one side to the leg on the other. Repeat.

SKEWERING GROUND MEAT KEBABS

1 Dampen your hands with water before handling the ground meat. Take a piece the size of an egg and mold it around the center of the skewer – flat blades are best (see page 148).

2 Moisten your hands again and then stretch out the mixture along the length of the skewer, lightly pressing it into shape, until you have a sausage about 4in (10cm) long.

The kebabs are now ready to be cooked in the broiler or on the grill. Cover with plastic wrap until needed.

STOCK

A stock is an infusion of flavors into a liquid, usually water. Fish, meat, and vegetable stocks are very basic descriptions: there is a great difference between a shellfish and a fish stock or a beef and a chicken stock. Stocks can be light or strong, depending on how much they have been reduced. It is worth making stock whenever you have excess vegetables, a few fish heads, or some bones. Stock freezes well and bouillon cubes are no replacement.

TO MAKE A STOCK
Place the fish or shellfish trimmings, vegetables, or meat bones in a pan and cover with water. Add flavorings such as herbs, spices, 1 or 2 glasses of wine, and onion, according to the main ingredient. Bring to a boil, then reduce to a slow simmer. Let cook uncovered. The longer the stock cooks, the more intense its flavor will be. If you wish to strengthen the flavor, boil hard to reduce it at the end of the simmering period. Always salt stock at the end of reducing – the saltiness is intensified as the stock reduces – and skim off any fat or impurities.

Fish stock should never be cooked for more than 40 minutes or it will become glue.

Meat stock will be more flavorful if the bones are first roasted.

Vegetable stock is improved if the vegetables are first sautéed in a very little oil.

NUTRITIONAL INFORMATION

RECIPE	KCAL	FAT (g)	SOD.	RECIPE	KCAL	FAT (g)	SOD.	RECIPE	KCAL	FAT (g)	SOD.
Ajo Blanco con Uvas	524	5(s) 36(u)	552	Fattoush	437	6(s) 32(u)	325	La Pizzaiola	421	10(s) 20(u)	506
Albondigas	552	12(s) 24(u)	522	Fish Plaki	804	8(s) 39(u)	1438	Poulet Sauté aux Herbes	800	11(s) 24(u)	699
Allioli	401	6(s) 37(u)	486	Flan de Naranja	300	4(s) 7(u)	140	Rahat Lokum	670	– 8(u)	6
Almejas a la Marinera	547	4(s) 21(u)	384	Foie de Veau aux Câpres	402	6(s) 17(u)	719	Ratatouille	533	7(s) 38(u)	399
Anchoïade	207	3(s) 17(u)	983	Fraises de Bois au Vin Rouge	148	–	20	Riñones al Jerez	210	3(s) 9(u)	367
Anginares me Koukia	263	3(s) 19(u)	305	Frittata di Zucchine	389	12(s) 16(u)	671	Risotto di Carciofi	477	18(s) 14(u)	754
Arni Frikase Avgolemono	602	20(s) 25(u)	901	Fritto Misto di Mare	588	6(s) 40(u)	1444	Romesco de Peix	898	7(s) 54(u)	681
Arrosta di Maiale	958	22(s) 40(u)	412	Ful Medames	185	2(s) 13(u)	212	Rougets à la Niçoise	1256	22(s) 69(u)	5985
Avgolemono Soupa	89	2(s) 4(u)	70	Gazpacho Andaluz	431	4(s) 20(u)	1332	Roz bi Saffran	306	9(s) 9(u)	408
Baba Ghanouj	277	4(s) 20(u)	154	Gnocchi al Pesto	808	11(s) 42(u)	1134	Salade d'Oranges	78	–	5
Baklava	1672	51(s) 65(u)	812	Granita di Cocomero	324	–	5	Salata Horiatiki	449	11(s) 31(u)	1091.
Beignets de Fleurs de Courgette	425	11(s) 21(u)	893	Habas con Jamon	442	5(s) 25(u)	757	Salata il Shamonder	280	3(s) 19(u)	416
Böreks	555	27(s) 20(u)	1029	Harira	105	1(s) 4(u)	273	Salata Jazar	181	2(s) 14(u)	357
Bouillabaisse	1121	12(s) 57(u)	1497	Huevos Revueltos	294	9(s) 16(u)	637	Salpicon de Mariscos	362	4(s) 21(u)	1988
Bourride	838	9(s) 39(u)	1306	Hummus bi Tahini	351	4(s) 26(u)	301	Samak Charmoula	542	6(s) 28(u)	1392
Brik à l'Oeuf	651	12(s) 39(u)	647	Iç Pilavi	471	16(s) 18(u)	517	Samak Meshwi bi Tahini	817	9(s) 46(u)	588
Bruschetta	295	2(s) 11(u)	506	Imam Bayildi	1024	15(s) 87(u)	551	Sardalya Sarmasi	330	6(s) 21(u)	931
Çaçik Soupa	231	4(s) 9(u)	153	Khoshaf	658	2(s) 23(u)	45	Sephardi Tamar	239	5(s) 9(u)	63
Calamares a la Plancha	205	2(s) 10(u)	512	Kiliç siste Tarator	860	11(s) 56(u)	994	Sika sto Fourno	90	–	8
Calamares Rellenos	571	5(s) 23(u)	1320	Kounelli Stifatho	1487	14(s) 72(u)	3295	Şiş Kebab	668	29(s) 31(u)	416
Canalons	785	21(s) 30(u)	891	Loup de Mer Grillé au Fenouil	386	4(s) 20(u)	463	Şiş Koftesi	609	28(s) 24(u)	418
Caponata	772	12(s) 67(u)	1236	Manitaria Afelia	164	2(s) 13(u)	200	Soumanate bi' Leinab	1074	17(s) 43(u)	1884
Capriolo in Agrodolce	642	4(s) 27(u)	552	Mejadarra	538	6(s) 33(u)	298	Soupe au Pistou	394	7(s) 22(u)	821
Carciofa alla Giudea	691	11(s) 64(u)	294	Mesclun	218	3(s) 19(u)	114	Soupe aux Moules	291	2(s) 12(u)	851
Cassoulet	1126	32(s) 59(u)	3248	Minestrone alla Livornese	260	5(s) 11(u)	1438	Soupe de Potiron	145	1(s) 4(u)	31
Chakchouka	265	5(s) 16(u)	337	Moussaka	566	17(s) 18(u)	790	Spaghetti alla Puttanesca	348	3(s) 19(u)	1626
Champiñones al Ajillo	155	2(s) 13(u)	200	Mozzarella in Carrozza	586	14(s) 24(u)	1856	Spanakopita	559	4(s) 24(u)	1264
Cipolline in Agrodolce	156	2(s) 11(u)	201	Oktapothi sti Skara	66	8(s) 4(u)	492	Tabbouleh	473	7(s) 38(u)	297
Coca Mallorquina	548	6(s) 21(u)	498	Orecchiette al Ragù	488	24(s) 36(u)	2307	Tagine d'Agneau aux Abricots	605	29(s) 24(u)	363
Coquilles St. Jacques	184	2(s) 13(u)	423	Osso Buco	888	8(s) 29(u)	814	Tapenade	447	6(s) 33(u)	1814
Couscous al Samak	320	5(s) 4(u)	1639	Paella Valenciana	806	11(s) 29(u)	1162	Tarte au Citron	821	23(s) 16(u)	502
Couscous aux Sept Légumes	389	7(s) 5(u)	457	Pan Bagnat	649	6(s) 22(u)	2270	Tian de Sardines	979	23(s) 47(u)	2702
Crostini di Fegato	539	11(s) 28(u)	647	Panzanella	355	3(s) 15(u)	692	Tortilla	576	8(s) 34(u)	715
Daoud Pasha	616	17(s) 29(u)	431	Parmigiana	519	17(s) 23(u)	1197	Tsatsiki	175	8(s) 4(u)	648
Daube de Boeuf	986	29(s) 42(u)	1184	Pasta e Fagioli	419	4(s) 16(u)	1431	Tumbet	752	10(s) 54(u)	1070
Djej Emshmel	560	7(s) 25(u)	1661	Pasta con le Sarde	846	9(s) 55(u)	1440	Uskumru Dolmasi	631	8(s) 33(u)	408
Djej Meshwi	1594	19(s) 54(u)	1238	Patatas Bravas	272	2(s) 13(u)	217	Yemistes Piperies	556	13(s) 26(u)	816
Dolmathes	640	7(s) 47(u)	393	Pato a la Sevillana	1837	43(s) 106(u)	1392	Yoğurtlu Kebab	1008	35(s) 48(u)	867
Dukkah	265	3(s) 21(u)	492	Peperonata	307	4(s) 22(u)	594	Yoğurtlu Patlican	432	7(s) 33(u)	360
Ensalada Sevillana	359	5(s) 30(u)	904	Peras Estofados	362	3(u)	18	Zuppa di Pesce	1356	21(s) 78(u)	2840
Escabeche	492	4(s) 26(u)	500	Pesce alla Griglia Salsa Verde	711	10(s) 54(u)	644				
Escalivada	269	3(s) 14(u)	306	Pesche Ripiene	157	2(s) 6(u)	38				
Espinacas a la Catalana	499	5(s) 32(u)	1137	Pinchos Morunos	498	7(s) 26(u)	417				
Esqueixada	493	5(s) 29(u)	1136	Pissaladière	1030	8(s) 48(u)	1403				
Falafel	129	1(s) 5(u)	489	Pizza alla Marinara	828	4(s) 24(u)	612				

KEY:

FAT: (s) = saturated fat (u) = unsaturated fat
SOD: sodium calculated in mg. (Half a teaspoon of salt assumed if no amount given.)
KCAL: energy/calories
Breakdowns are per serving. All recipes make 4 servings, unless otherwise indicated in text.

INDEX

Figures in **bold** refer to pages
with illustrations

A

aïoli, 96
Ajo Blanco con Uvas, 60
Albondigas, 110
Allioli, 66
Almejas a la Marinera, 90
almonds, **17**
  dried fruit and nut salad, 136
  iced almond soup with grapes, 60
  pilaf with chicken livers, **128**, 130
  romesco pepper sauce, **98-9**
  stuffed dates, 137
  stuffed peaches, **135**
Anchoïade, 67
anchovies, **18**, **31**
  anchovy paste, 67
  deep-fried mozzarella
    sandwiches, 71
  green sauce, **51**, 96
  red mullet Niçois style, **56-7**, **143**
  salade niçoise in a roll, **68-9**, **143**
  Sevillian salad, 76, **82**
  spaghetti with spicy sauce, 126
Andalusian gazpacho, **36-7**, **140**
Anginares me Koukia, 76
apricots, **17**
  dried fruit and nut salad, 136
  Moroccan rice with dried fruit and
    nuts, 46-**7**, 130
  Moroccan tagine of lamb with
    apricots, **118**
Arni Frikase Avgolemono, 111, **112**
Arrosta di Maiale, **113**, 114
artichokes, **13**
  artichoke risotto, 127
  artichokes Jewish style, 77, **83**
  marinated baby artichokes, 30
  preparing, **150**
  salad of artichokes with baby
    fava beans, 76
asparagus, **13**
  scrambled eggs with asparagus, 88
eggplant, **13**
  baked eggplant layered with
    lamb, 114
  baked vegetables, 89
  eggplant baked with mozzarella
    and Parmesan, 87, **144**
  fried eggplant with yogurt, 88
  purée of eggplant, **44**, 70, **140**
  roasted peppers, eggplant and
    onions, **83**, 88
  salting and blotting, **150**
  stuffed eggplant, **40-1**
  sweet and sour eggplant, onion,
    and celery salad, **78-9**
  vegetables stewed in olive oil, 81
Avgolemono Soupa, 65

B

Baba Ghanouj, **44**, 70,**142**
baked:
  eggplant layered with lamb, 114
  eggplant with mozzarella and
    Parmesan, 87, **144**
  figs, 134
  fish with vegetables, **104-5**
  orange custard, 137
  vegetables, 89

Baklava, 138, **142**
barbecue menu, 144
basil, **25**
  pesto sauce, **42-3**
  pistou sauce, 64
beans, **12**, **27**
  flageolets, 27
  pasta and beans, 123
  stewed beans, 70
  Valencian paella, **52-3**
  vegetable soup with pistou sauce,
    64
  white beans with pork and
    duck, 119
  see also borlotti beans, fava
    beans, white beans
beef, **23**
  beef casserole, **116-17**
  pasta with tomato sauce and
    meatballs, **124-5**
beet salad, 74
Beignets de Fleurs de Courgette, 84
Böreks, **45**, 72, **151**
borlotti beans, **27**
  pasta and beans, 123
  vegetable soup Livorno style, **62-3**
Bouillabaisse, **95**, 97
bouquet garni, 156
Bourride, 96
bread, 8, **26-7**
  bread and tomato salad, 120
  chicken liver toasts, 71
  country-style breads **27**
  deep-fried mozzarella
    sandwiches, 71
  dough, **151**
  focaccia , **26**
  garlic bread, 120
  Lebanese bread salad, 121
  olive oil bread, **27**
  pita bread, **26**
  salade niçoise in a roll, **68-9**, **143**
  sweet bread, **27**
Brik à l'Oeuf, 71
Bruschetta, 120
bulgur wheat, **26**
  bulgur wheat and herb salad, 130

C

cabbage, **15**
  vegetable soup Livorno style, **62-3**
Çaçik Soupa, 60
Calamares a la Plancha, 93
Calamares Rellenos, 102
calf's liver in tomato sauce
  with capers, 108
Canalons, 126, **128**
candied pumpkin, 132
cannelloni, **27**
  stuffed baked pasta, 126, **128**
capers, **30**
  calf's liver in tomato sauce
    with capers, 108
  green sauce, **51**, 96
  olive and caper paste, 66
  Sevillian salad, 76, **82**
Caponata, **78-9**
Capriolo in Agrodolce, 115
Carciofi alla Giudea, 77, **83**
carrots, **15**
  carrot salad, 74
  couscous with seven vegetables,
    129, 131

  vegetable soup Livorno style, **62-3**
casseroles:
  beef casserole, **116-17**
  Greek rabbit casserole, **54-5**
Cassoulet, 119
cauliflowers, **15**
  vegetable soup Livorno style, **62-3**
celery, **13**
  Provençal fish stew, 96
  sweet and sour eggplant, onion,
    and celery salad, **78-9**
cèpes, **14**, **30**
  beef casserole, **116-17**
Chakchouka, 81
Champiñones al Ajillo, **38**, 85
cheeses, **28-9**
chicken, **23**
  chicken sautéed with herbs
    and garlic in white wine, 111,
    113, **140**
  chicken soup with eggs and
    lemon, 65
  cutting up, **154**
  grilled spring chicken, **50**, 106
  paella, **52-3**
  splitting for grilling, **155**
  tagine of chicken with lemons
    and olives, **46-7**, **141**
chicken livers:
  chicken liver toasts, 71
  pilaf with chicken livers, **128**, 130
  stuffed baked pasta, 126, **128**
chickpeas, **27**
  chickpea fritters, **45**, 72
  chickpea and sesame dip, **44**, 70,
    142
  couscous with seven vegetables,
    129, 131
  fish couscous, 131
  Ramadan soup, 64
chilies:
  harissa, **30**
  romesco pepper sauce, **98-9**
  spaghetti with spicy sauce, 126
  spicy peppers and tomatoes with
    eggs, 81
chorizo, **22**
  Valencian paella, **52-3**
cilantro, **25**
  Ramadan soup, 64
  tagine of chicken with lemons
    and olives, **46-7**
Cipolline in Agrodolce, 80
clams, **20**
  clams with white wine and garlic
    sauce, 90
  Italian fish soup, **34-5**, **141**
  preparing, **153**
  seafood stew with romesco
    pepper sauce, **98-9**
  Spanish shellfish salad, **39**, **91**
  Valencian paella, **52-3**
Coca Mallorquina, 122
cocktail party menu, 145
cod:
  Provençal fish stew, 96
  salt cod salad, 90
cold soup of yogurt and cucumber, 60
Conserva di Peperoni, 132-3
Coquilles St. Jacques à la
  Provençale, **95**, 97
coriander seeds, **25**
  mushrooms in red wine with
    coriander seeds, 77

  roasted spice and nut mix, 67
couscous, **26**
  couscous with seven vegetables,
    129, 131
  fish couscous, 131
Couscous al Samak, 131
Couscous aux Sept Légumes, **129**,
  131
Crostini di Fegato, 71
cucumbers, **12**
  Andalusian gazpacho, **36-7**, **140**
  cold soup of yogurt and
    cucumber, 60
  Lebanese bread salad, 121
  peasant salad, 75, **144**
  salade niçoise in a roll, **68-9**, **143**
  yogurt and cucumber dip, **44**, 70
cumin, **25**
  roasted spice and nut mix, 67
custard, baked orange, 137

D

Daoud Pasha, 110
dates, **17**
  stuffed dates, 137
Daube de Boeuf, **116-17**
deep-fried:
  fish, 96
  mozzarella sandwiches, 71
dinner party menu, 145
Djej Emshmel, **46-7**, **141**
Djej Meshwi, **50**, 106
Dolmathes, **45**, 72-3
dough, making, **151**
dried fruit, **17**
  dried fruit and nut salad, 136
  Moroccan rice with dried fruit
    and nuts, 46-**7**, 130
duck, **23**
  duck with olives, orange, and
    sherry, 115
  white beans cooked with pork
    and duck, 119
Dukkah, 67
Dulce de Membrillo, 133

E

Eastern Mediterranean menu, 142
eggs:
  baked eggplant layered with
    lamb, 114
  baked orange custard, 137
  chicken soup with eggs and
    lemon, 65
  fried pastries with egg and tuna,
    71
  lamb fricassee with egg and
    lemon sauce, 111, **112**
  potato omelet, **39**, 85, **145**
  salade niçoise in a roll, **68-9**, **143**
  scrambled eggs with asparagus, 88
  Tunisian spicy peppers and
    tomatoes with eggs, 81
  zucchini omelet, 85
Egyptian roasted spice and nut
  mix, 67
Ensalada Sevillana, 76, **82**
equipment, **148-9**
Escabeche, 100
Escalivada, **83**, 88
Espinacas a la Catalana, **38**, 80
Esqueixada, 90

F

Falafel, **45**, 72
Fattoush, 121
fava beans, **12**, **27**
 couscous with seven vegetables, **129**, 131
 fava beans with ham, **39**, 80
 salad of artichokes with baby fava beans, 76
 stewed beans, 70
fennel, **13**
 pasta with sardines, 123
 Provençal fish stew, 96
 roast pork Italian style, **113**, 114
 sea bass grilled with fennel, 93
feta cheese, **29**
 peasant salad, **75**, **144**
 stuffed savory pastries, **45**, 72
figs, **17**
 baked figs, 134
fish, 9, **18-19**
 baked fish with vegetables, **104-5**
 broiled fish with sesame sauce, 92
 cleaning, **152**
 fish in aromatic vinegar, 100
 fish couscous, 131
 fish stock, 155
 Italian fish soup, **34-5**, **141**
 Italian grilled fish with green sauce, **51**, 96
 marinated and baked fish, 103
 Marseillais fish stew, **95**, 97
Fish Plaki, **104-5**
Flan de Naranja, 137
Foie de Veau aux Câpres, 108
Fraises de Bois au Vin Rouge, 136
fricassee of lamb with egg and lemon sauce, 111, **112**
Frittata di Zucchine, 85
Fritto Misto di Mare, 96
fruit, 8, **16-17**
Ful Medames, 70

G

garlic, 8, **30**
 chicken sautéed with herbs and garlic in white wine, 111, **113, 141**
 clams with white wine and garlic sauce, 90
 garlic bread, 120
 garlic and olive oil sauce, 66
 green sauce, **51**, 96
 spaghetti with spicy sauce, 126
 Spanish mushrooms with garlic, **38**, 85
Gazpacho Andaluz, **36-7**, **140**
gazpacho, white, 60
Gnocchi al Pesto, **42-3**
Granita di Cocomero, 139
grape leaves:
 stuffed, **45**, 72-3
 stuffed sardines in grape leaves, **94**, 102
 stuffing technique, **73**
grapes, **17**
 iced almond soup with grapes, 60
 quail with grapes, 109, **145**
gray mullet, **19**
 broiled fish with sesame sauce, 92
 fish baked with vegetables, **104-5**
 fish couscous, 131
 Italian fish soup, **34-5**, **141**
Greek:
 menu, 142
 rabbit casserole, **54-5**

Gremolada, 119
grilled/broiled food, **50-1**
 broiled fish with sesame sauce, 92
 grilled octopus, 93
 grilled spring chicken, **50**, 106
 grilled squid, 93
 ground meat on skewers, **50**, 106, **155**
 Italian grilled fish with green sauce, **51**, 96
 lamb kebabs, **51**, 107
 lamb kebabs with yogurt, 107
 pork kebabs, **38**, 107
 sea bass grilled with fennel, 93
 stuffed sardines in grape leaves, **94**, 102
ground meat on skewers, **50**, 106, **155**

H

Habas con Jamon, **39**, 80
ham, **22**
 fava beans with ham, **39**, 80
 pasta and beans, 123
 stuffed squid, 102
Harira, 64
harissa, **30**
 couscous with seven vegetables, **129**, 131
 Ramadan soup, 64
hazelnuts:
 Moroccan rice with dried fruit and nuts, 46-**47**, 130
 roasted spice and nut mix, 67
 romesco pepper sauce, **98-9**
herbs, **24-5**
 chicken sautéed with herbs and garlic in white wine, 111, **113, 140**
honey, **31**
 baked figs, 134
 Greek rabbit casserole, **54-5**
 pastry with nuts, 138, **142**
 poached pears, 134
 sweet and sour baby onions, 80
 venison in a sweet and sour sauce, 115
Huevos Revueltos con Esparragos, 88
Hummus bi Tahini, **44**, 70, **142**

I·J·K

Iç Pilavi, **128**, 130
iced almond soup with grapes, 60
Imam Bayildi, **40-1**
Italian:
 fish soup, **34-5**, **141**
 grilled fish with green sauce, **51**, 96
 menu, 141
 roast pork, **113**, 114
kebabs:
 ground meat on skewers, **50**, 106, **155**
 lamb, **51**, 107
 lamb with yogurt, 107
 pork, **38**, 107
 preparing, **155**
 swordfish, **51**, 92
Khoshaf, 136
kidneys cooked in sherry, 108
Kiliç siste Tarator, **51**, 92
Kounelli Stifatho, **54-5**

L

lamb, **23**
 baked eggplant layered with

 lamb, 114
 fricassee of lamb with egg and lemon sauce, 111, **112**
 ground meat on skewers, **50**, 106, **153**
 lamb kebabs, **51**, 107
 lamb kebabs with yogurt, 107
 Moroccan tagine of lamb with apricots, **118**
 Ramadan soup, 64
 spicy lamb meatballs with pine nuts in tomato sauce, 110
 stuffed peppers with tomato sauce, 86
Lebanese:
 bread salad, 121
 eggplant and sesame dip, **44**, 70
leeks, **14**
 vegetable soup Livorno style, **62-3**
 vegetable soup with pistou sauce, 64
legumes, 8, **26-7**
lemons, **16**
 chicken soup with eggs and lemon, 65
 fricassee of lamb with egg and lemon sauce, 111, **112**
 lemon tart, 136
 preserved lemons, 46-7, **133**
 tagine of chicken with lemons and olives, 46-7, **141**
lentils, 8, **27**
 Ramadan soup, 64
 rice with lentils and onions, 127
lettuces, **12-13**
 fricassee of lamb with egg and lemon sauce, 111, **112**
 Lebanese bread salad, 121
 peasant salad, 75, **144**
 Sevillian salad, 76, **82**
Loup de Mer Grillé au Fenouil, 93

M

mackerel, 9, **19**
 Italian fish soup, **34-5**, **141**
 stuffed mackerel, 100
 stuffing technique, **101**
Majorcan-style pizza, 122
Manchego cheese, **28**
Manitaria Afelia, 77
marinated:
 baked fish, 103
 olives, **133**
Marseillais fish stew, **95**, 97
meat, 9, **22-3**
 ground meat on skewers, **50**, 106, **155**
 stock, 153
meatballs:
 pasta with tomato sauce and meatballs, **124-5**
 pork and parsley meatballs, 110
 spicy lamb meatballs with pine nuts in tomato sauce, 110
Mejadarra, 127
menus, 140-5
Mesclun, 77
meze, **44-5**
Minestrone alla Livornese, **62-3**
mint, **24**
 bulgur wheat and herb salad, 130
 yogurt and cucumber dip, **44**, 70
monkfish, **19**
 Italian fish soup, **34-5**, **141**
 Marseillais fish stew, **95**, 97
 Provençal fish stew, 96
 seafood stew with romesco pepper sauce, **98-9**

Moroccan rice with dried fruit and nuts, 46-7, 130
Moroccan tagine of lamb with apricots, **118**
Moussaka, 114
mozzarella, **29**
 deep-fried mozzarella sandwiches, 71
 eggplant baked with mozzarella and Parmesan, **87**, **144**
Mozzarella in Carrozza, 71
mullet, *see* gray mullet, red mullet
mushrooms, **14**
 dried wild, **30**
 mushrooms in red wine with coriander seeds, 77
 preparing, 150
 Spanish mushrooms with garlic, **38**, 85
mussels, **20**
 Italian fish soup, **34-5**, **141**
 mussel soup, 65
 preparing, **153**
 Spanish shellfish salad, **39**, 91

N·O

North African menu, 141
nuts, **17**
 dried fruit and nut salad, 136
 Moroccan rice with dried fruit and nuts, 46-**47**, 130
 pastry with nuts, **138**, **142**
octopus, grilled, 93
Oktapothi sti Skara, 93
olive oil, 8, **31**
 garlic and olive oil sauce, 66
 stuffed eggplant, **40-1**
olives, **31**
 duck with olives, orange, and sherry, 115
 marinated olives, **133**
 olive and caper paste, 66
 peasant salad, **75**, **144**
 Provençal onion tart, **48-9**
 red mullet Niçois style, **56-7**, **143**
 salade niçoise in a roll, **68-9**, **143**
 Sevillian salad, 76, **82**
 tagine of chicken with lemons and olives, 46-7, **141**
omelet:
 Spanish potato, **39**, 85, **145**
 zucchini, 85
onions, **14**
 Greek rabbit casserole, **54-5**
 Provençal onion tart, **48-9**
 rice with lentils and onions, 127
 roasted peppers, eggplant, and onions, **83**, 88
 sweet and sour baby onions, 80
 sweet and sour eggplant, onion, and celery salad, **78-9**
 vegetables stewed in olive oil, 81
oranges, **16**
 baked orange custard, 137
 duck with olives, orange, and sherry, 115
 orange salad, 136
 Sevillian salad, 76, **82**
orecchiette, **27**
 pasta with tomato sauce and meatballs, **124-5**
Orecchiette al Ragù, **124-5**
Osso Buco, 119

P

Paella Valenciana, **52-3**
Pan Bagnat, **68-9**, **143**

pancetta, **22**
  vegetable soup Livorno style, **62-3**
  white beans cooked with pork
    and duck, 119
Panzanella, 120
Parmesan, **29**
  eggplant baked with mozzarella
    and Parmesan, **87**, **144**
  pesto sauce, **42-3**
  sardines baked with Swiss chard,
    spinach, and Parmesan, 103
Parmigiana, **87**, **144**
parsley, **25**
  bulgur wheat and herb salad, 130
  green sauce, **51**, 96
  pork and parsley meatballs, 110
  Ramadan soup, 64
  tagine of chicken with lemon and
    olives, **46-7**
pasta, 8-9, **27**
  pasta and beans, 123
  pasta with sardines, 123
  pasta with tomato sauce and
    meatballs, **124-5**
  stuffed baked pasta, 126, **128**
Pasta e Fagioli, 123
Pasta con le Sarde, 123
pastes:
  anchovy paste, 67
  olive and caper paste, 66
  quince paste, 133
pastries:
  fried pastries with egg and tuna,
    71
  pastry with nuts, **138**, **142**
  stuffed savory pastries, **45**, 72,
    151
Patatas Bravas, 84
Pato a la Sevillana, 115
peaches, **16**
  stuffed peaches, **135**
pears, poached, 134
peas:
  couscous with seven vegetables,
    129, 131
  Valencian Paella, **52-3**
peasant salad, **75**, **144**
Pecorino Sardo, **29**
  pesto sauce, **42-3**
Peperonata, 80
peppers, **13**
  Andalusian gazpacho, **36-7**, **140**
  baked fish with vegetables, **104-5**
  baked vegetables, 89
  bottled red pimiento, **30**
  peeling, **150**
  preserved peppers, 132-3
  roasted peppers, eggplant, and
    onions, **83**, 88
  stewed peppers, 80
  stuffed peppers with tomato
    sauce, **86**
  Tunisian spicy peppers and
    tomatoes with eggs, 81
  vegetables stewed in olive oil, 81
Peras Estofados, 134
Pesce alla Griglia Salsa Verde, **51**, 96
Pesche Ripiene, **135**
pesto sauce, **42-3**
phyllo pastry:
  fried pastries with egg and tuna, 71
  making bundles, **151**
  pastry with nuts, **138**, **142**
  stuffed savory pastries, **45**, 72,
    151
pickles and preserves, **30**, **132-3**
picnic menu, 143
pilaf with chicken livers, **128**, 130
Pinchos Morunos, **38**, 107

pine nuts, **17**
  pasta with sardines, 123
  pesto sauce, **42-3**
  pilaf with chicken livers, **128**, 130
  Moroccan rice with dried fruit
    and nuts, **46-7**, 130
  spicy lamb meatballs with pine
    nuts, 110
Pissaladière, **48-9**
pistachio nuts:
  pastry with nuts, 138, **142**
  stuffed dates, 137
  Turkish delight, 137
pistou sauce, 64
pita bread, **26**
  lamb kebabs with yogurt, 107
  Lebanese bread salad, 121
pizza, Majorcan-style, **122**
Pizza alla Marinara, 121
pizza with tomato sauce, 121
Pizzaiola, La, 108
poached pears, 134
porcini mushrooms, see cèpes
pork, 22
  pasta with tomato sauce and
    meatballs, **124-5**
  pork and parsley meatballs, 110
  pork kebabs, **38**, 107
  roast pork Italian style, **113**, 114
  stuffed baked pasta, 126, **128**
  white beans with pork and
    duck, 119
potatoes:
  baked vegetables, 89
  Italian potato dumplings with
    pesto sauce, **42-3**
  Spanish potato omelette, **39**, 85,
    145
  spicy potatoes, 84
Poulet Sauté aux Herbes de
  Provence, 111, **113**
preserves, **30**, **132-3**
  preserved lemons, **46-7**, **133**
  preserved peppers, **132-3**
prosciutto, **22**
  pasta and beans, 123
  vegetable soup Livorno style, **62-3**
Provençal:
  fish stew, 96
  menu, 140
  onion tart, **48-9**
  zucchini flower fritters with
    fresh tomato sauce, 84
pumpkin, **15**
  candied pumpkin, 132
  couscous with seven vegetables,
    129, 131
  pumpkin soup, **61**

Q·R

quail, **23**
  quail with grapes, **109**, **145**
quince, **17**
  quince paste, 133
rabbit casserole, **54-5**
Rahat Lokum, 137
raisins, **17**
  couscous with seven vegetables,
    129, 131
  dried fruit and nut salad, 136
  Moroccan rice with dried fruit
    and nuts, **46-7**, 130
  spinach Catalan style, **38**, 80
  stuffed mackerel, 100
Ramadan soup, 64
Ratatouille, 81
red mullet, **19**
  fish couscous, 131

Italian fish soup, **34-5**, **141**
Italian grilled fish with green
  sauce, **51**, 96
Marseillais fish stew, **95**, 97
red mullet Niçois style, **56-7**, **143**
rice, 8, **26**
  artichoke risotto, 127
  Moroccan rice with dried fruits
    and nuts, **46-7**, 130
  pilaf with chicken livers, **128**, 130
  rice with lentils and onions, 127
  sardines baked with Swiss chard,
    spinach and Parmesan, 103
  stuffed grape leaves, **45**, 72
  stuffed peppers with tomato
    sauce, **86**
  stuffed squid, 102
  Valencian paella, **52-3**
Riñones al Jerez, 108
risotto, artichoke, 127
Risotto di Carciofi, 127
roast pork Italian style, **113**, 114
roasted:
  peppers, eggplant, and onions,
    83, 88
  spice and nut mix, 67
Romesco de Peix, **98-9**
Rouget à la Niçoise, **56-7**, **143**
Rouille, **95**, 97
Roz bi Saffran, **46-7**, 130

S

saffron, **25**
  Moroccan rice with dried fruit
    and nuts, 46-7,130
salads:
  artichokes with baby fava
    beans, 76
  beet, 74
  bread and tomato, 120
  bulgur wheat and herb, 130
  carrot, 74
  dried fruit and nut, 136
  Lebanese bread, 121
  orange, 136
  peasant, **75**, **144**
  salade niçoise in a roll, **68-9**, **143**
  salt cod, 90
  Sevillian, 76, **82**
  Spanish shellfish, **39**, **91**
  sweet and sour eggplant, onion,
    and celery, **78-9**
  young leaves, 77
Salade d'Oranges, 136
Salata Horiatiki, **75**, **144**
Salata Jazar, 74
Salata il Shamonder, 74
Salpicon de Mariscos, **39**, **91**
Salsa Verde, **51**, 96
salt cod salad, 90
salting and blotting, 150
Samak Charmoula, 103
Samak Meshwi bi Tahini, 92
Sardalaya Sarmasi, **94**, 102
sardines, **18**
  Italian fish soup, **34-5**, **141**
  pasta with sardines, 123
  sardines baked with Swiss chard,
    spinach, and Parmesan, 103
  stuffed sardines in grape leaves,
    94, 102
sauces:
  fresh tomato, 84
  green, **51**, 96
  pesto, **42-3**
  pistou, 64
  romesco pepper, **98-9**
  sesame, 92

walnut, **51**, 92
sausages, **22-3**
  white beans cooked with pork
    and duck, 119
scallions, **14**
  Lebanese bread salad, 121
  peasant salad, **75**, **144**
  salad of artichokes with baby
    fava beans, 76
scallops, **20**
  cleaning, **153**
  Italian fish soup, **34-5**, **141**
  scallops with garlic and Cognac,
    95, 97
scrambled egg with asparagus, 88
sea bass, **18**
  broiled fish with sesame sauce, 92
  fish cooked in aromatic vinegar,
    100
  fish couscous, 131
  marinated and baked fish, 103
  Provençal fish stew, 96
  sea bass grilled with fennel, 93
  seafood stew with romesco
    pepper sauce, **98-9**
sea bream, **19**
  baked fish with vegetables,
    104-5
  broiled fish with sesame sauce, 92
  fish cooked in aromatic vinegar,
    100
  fish couscous, 131
  Italian fish soup, **34-5**, **141**
  Provençal fish stew, 96
  seafood stew with romesco
    pepper sauce, **98-9**
Sephardi Tamar, 137
Serrano ham, **22**
  fava beans with ham, **39**, 80
  stuffed squid, 102
sesame:
  broiled fish with sesame sauce, 92
  chickpea and sesame dip, **44**, 70,
    140
  eggplant and sesame dip, **44**,
    70, 140
  roasted spice and nut mix, 67
  tahini paste, **30**
Sevillian salad, 76, **82**
shellfish, 9, **20-1**
  cleaning, **153**
  Spanish shellfish salad, **39**, **91**
sherry:
  duck with olives, orange, and
    sherry, 115
  kidneys cooked in sherry, 108
  poached pears, 134
shrimp, **21**
  deep-fried fish, 96
  Italian fish soup, **34-5**, **141**
  Spanish shellfish salad, **39**, **91**
Sika sto Fourno, 134
Şiş Kebab, **51**, 107
Şiş Köftesi, **50**, 106, **155**
Soumanate bi' Leinab, **109**, **145**
Soupe aux Moules, 65
Soupe au Pistou, 64
Soupe de Potiron, 61
soups, 60-6
  Andalusian gazpacho, **36-7**, **140**
  chicken soup with eggs and
    lemon, 65
  cold yogurt and cucumber soup,
    60
  iced almond soup with grapes, 60
  Italian fish soup, **34-5**, **141**
  mussel soup, 65
  pumpkin soup, **61**
  Ramadan soup, 64

soups continued
vegetable soup Livorno style, **62-3**
vegetable soup with pistou
sauce, 64
spaghetti, **27**
pasta and beans, 123
spaghetti with spicy sauce, 126
Spaghetti alla Puttanesca, 126
Spanakopita, 89
Spanish:
menu, 140
mushrooms with garlic, **38**, 85
potato omelet, **39**, 85, **145**
shellfish salad, **39**, **91**
spices, 24-5
spinach, **15**
sardines baked with Swiss chard,
spinach, and Parmesan, 103
spinach Catalan style, **38**, 80
spinach pie, 89
squid, **20**
deep-fried fish, 96
grilled squid, 93
Italian fish soup, **34-5**, **141**
preparing, **153**
stuffed squid, 102
steak with tomato sauce, 108
stewed:
beans, 70
peppers, 80
shin of veal, 119
stocks, 155
strawberries, wild, **16**
Provençal wild strawberries in
red wine, 136
stuffed:
baked pasta, 126, **128**
dates, 137
eggplant, **40-1**
grape leaves, **45**, 72-3
mackerel, 100-1
peaches, **135**
peppers with tomato sauce, **86**
sardines in grape leaves, **94**, 102
savory pastries, **45**, 72, **151**
squid, 102
summer lunch menu, 143
supper menu, 144
sweet and sour:
baby onions, 80
eggplant, onion, and celery
salad, 78-9
venison in a sweet and sour
sauce, 115
Swiss chard:
sardines baked with Swiss chard,

spinach, and Parmesan, 103
vegetable soup with pistou
sauce, 64
swordfish, **19**
fish cooked in aromatic vinegar,
100
seafood stew with romesco
pepper sauce, **98-9**
swordfish kebabs with walnut
sauce, **51**, 92

—————— T ——————

Tabbouleh, 130
Tagine d'Agneau aux Abricots, 118
tagine of chicken with lemons and
olives, **46-7**, **141**
tagine of lamb with apricots, 118
tahini paste, 30
broiled fish with sesame sauce, 92
chickpea and sesame dip, **44**,
70, **140**
eggplant and sesame dip, **44**,
70, **140**
tapas, 38-9
Tapenade, 66
Tarator sauce, **51**, 92
Tarte au Citron, 136
Tian de Sardines, 103
tomatoes, **12**, 30
Andalusian gazpacho, **36-7**, **140**
baked vegetables, 89
bread and tomato salad, 120
calf's liver in tomato sauce with
capers, 108
eggplant baked with mozzarella
and Parmesan, **87**, **144**
lamb kebabs with yogurt, 107
pasta with tomato sauce and
meatballs, **124-5**
paste, 30
peeling, **150**
pizza with tomato sauce, 121
salade niçoise in a roll, **68-9**,
143
steak with tomato sauce, 108
stewed peppers, 80
stuffed eggplant, **40-1**
stuffed peppers with tomato
sauce, **86**
stuffed squid, 102
sweet and sour eggplant, onion,
and celery salad, **78-9**
tomato sauce, 108, 121
Tunisian spicy peppers and
tomatoes with eggs, 81

vegetable soup Livorno style, **62-3**
vegetable soup with pistou sauce,
64
vegetables stewed in olive oil, 81
zucchini flower fritters with
fresh tomato sauce, **84**
Tortilla, **39**, 85, **145**
Tsatsiki, **44**, 70
Tumbet, 89
tuna, **19**
fish cooked in aromatic vinegar,
100
fried pastries with egg and tuna,
71
salade niçoise in a roll, **68-9**, **143**
Tunisian spicy peppers and
tomatoes with eggs, 81
Turkish:
delight, 137
menu, 142
pastries, **45**, 72
swordfish kebabs with walnut
sauce, **51**, 92
turnips, **15**
couscous with seven vegetables,
129, 131
fish couscous, 131
Tuscan chicken liver toasts, 71

—————— U·V ——————

Uskumru Dolmasi, 100
Valencian Paella, **52-3**
veal, **23**
stewed shin of veal, 119
vegetables, 6-7, 8, **12-15**
baked fish with vegetables, **104-5**
baked vegetables, 89
couscous with seven vegetables,
129, 131
stock, 155
vegetable soup Livorno style,
62-3
vegetable soup with pistou sauce,
64
vegetables stewed in olive oil, 81
venison, **23**
venison in a sweet and sour
sauce, 115
vermicelli:
mussel soup, 65
pumpkin soup, 61
vinegar, **31**
fish cooked in aromatic vinegar,
100
Greek rabbit casserole, **54-5**

sweet and sour baby onions, 80
sweet and sour eggplant, onion,
and celery salad, **78-9**
venison in a sweet and sour
sauce, 115

—————— W·Y·Z ——————

walnuts, **17**
pastry with nuts, **138**, 142
stuffed mackerel, 100-1
walnut sauce, **51**, 92
watermelon, **17**
granita, 139
white beans, **27**
vegetable soup with pistou
sauce, 64
white beans cooked with pork
and duck, 119
whitebait, **19**
deep-fried fish, 96
wild strawberries in red wine, 136
wine, 8, **31**
baked figs, 134
chicken sautéed with herbs and
garlic in white wine, 111,
113, **140**
clams with white wine and garlic
sauce, 90
Greek rabbit casserole, **54-5**
mushrooms in red wine with
coriander seeds, 77
Provençal wild strawberries in
red wine, 136
roast pork Italian style, **113**, 114
stuffed peaches, 135
Yemistes Piperies, 86
yogurt, 9, 28-9
cold soup of yogurt and
cucumber, 60
fried eggplant with yogurt, 88
Greek yogurt and cucumber dip,
44, 70
lamb kebabs with yogurt, 107
Yoğurtlu Kebab, 107
Yoğurtlu Patlican, 88
zucchinis, **12**
couscous with seven vegetables,
129, 131
vegetable soup with pistou
sauce, 64
vegetables stewed in olive oil, 81
zucchini flower fritters with fresh
tomato sauce, 84
zucchini omelet, 85
Zuppa di Pesce, **34-5**, **141**

ACKNOWLEDGMENTS

Author's acknowledgments
With grateful thanks to my parents for introducing me to the food and way of life of the Mediterranean at an early age; to my husband Jonathan for sharing with me a passion for the region and its cooking; and above all to the many people who over the years have taken me into their kitchens and generously given me their family recipes. And of course special thanks to Clive Streeter, Janice Murfitt, and Dave King, and all the team at Dorling Kindersley, especially Lorna and Jo, for their hard work in making the book look so splendid.

Dorling Kindersley would like to thank Clive Streeter for his generous help and enthusiasm and Janice Murfitt, our home economist, for her hard work. Special thanks also to home economists Deborah Greatrex, Sunil Vijayakar, Kerenza Harries and Kathy Man; Alison Stace for hand modeling; Ruth Ash for the nutritional breakdowns; Hilary Guy and Ayisha de Lanerolle for styling assistance; Artemi Kyriacou for photographic assistance; Sarah Ereira for the index; Amanda Ursell for nutritional advice; Sasha Kennedy and Emy Mamby for design assistance.
With thanks to the following companies and individuals for their assistance: The National Fruit Collection, Brogdale; Cool Chile Company; Steve Hatt, Lina Stores, Randall & Aubin, and Hyams and Cockerton, London. Many thanks to the following for kindly loaning equipment and props: Elizabeth David Cookshop, The Kasbah and Pages Catering Equipment, London; Mr. H. Leatherland.
Picture credits: Photography by Clive Streeter except Dave King: pages 2-3, 12-21, 23, 24-29, 55, 135, 140bl.